In a correspondence course programme
the YWCA of Australia
invited women over seventy
to write about their lives.
Some of the stories sent in
form this collection.

YESTERDAY'S
DAUGHTERS

YESTERDAY'S DAUGHTERS

Stories of our past by women over 70

Edited by
Alma Bushell

NELSON

For our families

Nelson Publishers
Thomas Nelson Australia
480 La Trobe Street Melbourne Victoria 3000

First published 1986
Copyright © Alma Bushell 1986

National Library of Australia
Cataloguing-in-Publication data:

Yesterday's daughters.

ISBN 0 17 006767 X.

1. Women — Australia — Biography. 2. Women — Australia
— Social conditions. I. Bushell, Alma.

305.4'0994

Typeset in 12/13 Baskerville by Abb-typesetting Pty Ltd
Printed in Australia by The Dominion Press/Hedges & Bell.

Contents

Introduction

Write about Your Life:
A correspondence course for people over 70

IT was only a chance remark that mooted the idea of a course specially for the over seventies, and simply coincidental that no men applied. At the time it seemed there were few programmes, social or educational, that addressed themselves specifically to the needs and capabilities of this group. Older people need contact, camaraderie, stimulation and a feeling of individual worth, the same almost as anyone, except that they are more likely to have physical limitations — less mobility, health problems, and often isolation through the death of a partner or distance from other family members. They are left with 'What we have now is all we can hope to have, so what can we do with it?' It is a basic and imperative question.

In the beginning everyone approached the course tentatively. At the 'Y', when we advertised in the national papers, we had no idea of the form it would take. And indeed, the course was made up as we went along, given direction by the interests of the writers themselves. All applicants were cautious about their abilities, from Ivy who apologised, 'I can't spell', to Lady P. (MA Melb.) who afterwards wrote, 'I am so glad I had the courage to apply.'

Most wrote for their families; a few were ambitious, openly declaring they had 'always wanted to write a book'. (And who has not?)

Educational backgrounds, from Primary grade 6 upwards, had nothing to do with creative energy as it stirred. Reams and reams and reams of writing poured in. We wished we had set a limit. But once writing was so joyously under way, how could we stop them?

And joy it was. Everyone seemed caught up in a singing. It was a feeling of doing something they had always wanted to do, yet it was more than that. From eager reminiscence they reached deeper into long-forgotten, painful memories. The cathartic effect of revealing to themselves the unhappiness they had repressed, the hostilities, angers, jealousies, frustrations they had denied, improved their *health*!

Most of all, they saw at the end that they had an identity of their own, that their lives had had a value; and not only had they given shape to the past but were happily appraising the content and possibilities in the present.

Florence, whose husband Cecil died a few months after she had finished her story, later wrote:

'. . . We all miss him still but the family have made me realise that life doesn't stand still because of grief. One way they did this was to hand me a book, *Learner Drivers Permit Test*. I must explain — we live 11 km from Timboon, I have never driven before, and being seventy-five thought that I would never learn the answers to 231 questions — but with children and grandchildren prodding and tutoring I managed to get 'L' plates.

'My first driving lesson was in a large paddock, and even there the trees and stumps seemed to pop up in front of the car, but thanks to Del and Jean — who gave up their time to take me out on the roads — *I have my 'P' plates now.*'

Putting together these stories has been difficult. What were initially names on application forms have become whole lives inextricably woven into mine, more intimately connected than people I see every day. Submerged in their writings I feel I have lived their combined thousand and more years. Deeply moved by the simplicity of the words, the details so unselfconsciously revealed, I learn about my own life and an affinity grows in shared memories. The letters keep coming, confidences are made and sometimes I, too, unburden in reply.

Each story has been chosen to depict certain aspects of Australian women's lives this century. Of course it is far from comprehensive — the variety of individual lives is infinite. But our emotions are fundamental, so is the spirit of courage, compassion and humour.

There were so many demands on my time through family, household, social and community commitments (without an identifiable paid job one seems to have to be always available) that the project begun so enthusiastically became unmanageable. The hours spent tutoring correspondence lessons, the tedium of sorting out the handwritten papers — transcribing, selecting and typing them, writing and answering so many letters, began to defeat me. It was time to give up.

And it was just then that a poem arrived in the mail from Eileen, dated on the anniversary of the death of my son. Shakily her arthritic hand had written:

> Dear Alma, do not weep and sigh
> (I know you do and so do I).
> We all must die, some young some later on
> But none is missed and loved more dearly
>   than a daughter or a son.
> A child is such a part of one that
> Time can never heal the void and yet
> We should count our blessings
> Even though as years go by
> We cannot forget.

Yes, Eileen, count them and create them too, as you all have done these many years.

'Life doesn't stand still because of grief.' No, indeed. But it may seem so, and we can become very lonely travellers in a

3

world that appears to rush by minding its own business.

The great crises of life exempt no-one. Sooner or later we face things we never dreamed could happen to us. Where are the maps, we would like to know, that show us where to go now? Who has been here before? Who can tell me what happens next? How will it all turn out? Is there one loving touch that can say, 'I have been there, I know how it feels'?

So it has been with *Yesterday's Daughters*. Look through the photographs, see the mischievous smile of a child, the happy sometimes serious young woman open to her future, then the careworn lines and maturity of middle age clearly showing the responsibilities that have taken over.

Yet there is a marvellous feeling of affinity, matching portraits with stories. This girl belongs here, this woman there. So closely had I identified with the lives of the writers in the periods they wrote about that it seemed the boundaries of my own experience had extended and I had become part of *their* reality. I recognised people and events as through the lens of my own camera.

Meeting them, poring over the albums together, there existed no separateness. It was almost like a religious experience, a feeling of oneness without barriers, because we had shared so much that was intimate. And perhaps barriers are created between us all because we imagine we are so different from each other, thinking sometimes that others are more than we are, and sometimes, too, that they are less.

The appealing child that grew into the handsome young woman (and some I thought were absolutely beautiful) who with the passing of years became the whole person before me, must have changed my very idea of beauty, for each lived-in face appeared illumined from within. I couldn't help thinking how much lovelier they now seemed.

Sandy's gentleness, Ivy's twinkling humorous eyes, Ethel's bright zest and vitality ('I am always cast as the crotchety old lady in our amateur plays'), Stella's eager observations and philosophies of life, and Alice telling me matter-of-factly, 'I'm nearly completely blind now, you know' — Alice who had once delicately corrected an indiscretion, 'Oh, I do not think of myself as an octogenarian, I am myself just as I have always been' — will remain forever to me indelible portraits of the daughters of yesterday.

Memoir and oral histories are personal recollections and as such cannot claim to be without flaws in accuracy. Wherever possible I have checked dates, figures, names and events but may still have overlooked some detail factually incorrect.

Our view of the historical past can only ever be impressionistic, the impression itself shifting as the light falls, now here, now there. However the spirit or climate of a period may be apprehended by the study of common experience within it — the spirit of unity that holds a people together, rather than a disintegration through destructive sources. Mateship is an example of this. In the women the unity is less obvious — perhaps because, in fact, their common lot is taken for granted.

Overall I have tried to evoke a view of life as it has happened to Australian women in the first half of this century — not all are Australian-born. Nor is it meant to be all-inclusive. Aboriginal and European migrant women have their own special stories to tell. There is so much still left to be written.

During the publishing process a great deal of curiosity stirred, for the things that are taken for granted are not written about. Questions kept cropping up — so much has changed in this technological age. The advent of television, mass ownership of motor cars, air travel, labour-saving appliances in the home, general affluence and social security, and not least the introduction of the Pill, mean that an era has passed within one generation. Students of history and sociology will find this a rich area to explore.

By understanding the conditions of the recent past and the attitudes, character and reasons of those who were part of it, we can begin to appraise our own. There was hardship, courage, resilience and rejoicing in these lives and we can take pride in what they reveal as well as hope for what can be made possible. We are a part of all that has gone before.

To maintain a consistency of values and terms with the historical period, imperial currency and measures have been retained. Some metrification equivalents are given in brackets. Similarly, meanings of words no longer in use are also bracketed. To make these kind of comparisons is to uncover a rewarding source of information.

ACKNOWLEDGEMENTS

I wish to thank the YWCA of Australia for making possible the project Write About Your Life, and in particular Amy Young, the course co-ordinator, whose experience, advice and encouragement was invaluable. I acknowledge gratefully the work of all the volunteer tutors without whose participation the course could not have proceeded; the Nasebandt family for permission to include Janet Nasebandt's poem, 'Washing Day — Three Generations'.

Alma Bushell

Ethel

Ethel Beed b.1904

MY mother, the eldest of four (two girls and two boys) whose own mother was widowed at thirty-three, had to leave school at thirteen. (She was a very good scholar and would have gone far if given the chance.) However, she was sent to learn tailoring and had to work six months for no pay, then got 2*s* 6*d* a week for the next six months. She married my father at the age of eighteen, he being only a year older. They did not set up their own home but, as was often done then (1899), combined with my grandma and her family. The elder of the two brothers married and moved out but the two youngest, brother and sister, never married and thus were part of our 'family' all my single life.

My mother was twenty when my elder sister Dorothy was born, and her mother was just twenty years older than she was. Two and a half years later I was born, which made the family total seven. My grandmother was always the matriarch. She was a very little woman, and was very kind and good, always doing something for those in need, but we always had to be very careful that our behaviour did not offend her.

My grandmother had had a hard battle to bring up her four children after her husband died. There was no government help for widows then, unless the children were 'put on the state' in which case they would all have been separated. My grandmother would not agree to this but preferred to work to keep them. She had not been taught a trade as she had seven brothers and the girls in this family were kept home to help. Her father was a tailor, and worked at home so she learnt needlework from him and did 'outdoor work' for which she received a very small remuneration. She told me that one Monday morning, after paying her rent, she had only 4½d in her purse, so she walked to a clothing factory a couple of miles away and collected a parcel of 'outdoor sewing'. She brought this home, did the sewing, and carried it back to the factory where she received a few shillings which enabled her to buy food for the next couple of days.

My earliest recollection is of when I was three. We lived in Camperdown (Sydney) in a terrace house of five rooms. We only had a woodfire stove and a gas ring for cooking, and gas for lighting in the downstairs while candles were used in the bedrooms.

One day my mother was bending down to the oven when I fell over her feet and burnt both my arms on the stove, from wrist to elbow. My mother carried me across to the casualty department of the Children's Hospital adjoining us. My arms were dressed on the end of a large seat, the other end of which was occupied by a child from whose throat a swab was being taken. Result: shortly afterwards I contracted diphtheria. I was taken to the Coast Hospital (now Prince Henry's) by horse-drawn ambulance.

Upon arrival at Little Bay (next to Long Bay where the gaol is) the children were all given an anti-toxin injection in the abdomen, and loud were the screams — which of course set off all the other children. We had to remain in the hospital until we were double negative, that is, two successive swabs had to be negative. It was often several weeks before we were allowed to go home. After we were allowed out of bed, however, we had rather a good time. Though confined to the ward, we had games and sing-songs and were happy and well cared for.

On visiting days, Sundays and Wednesdays, the children's beds were carried out on to a long verandah by wardsmen.

The parents had to stand outside a cyclone fence separated from the verandah by a lawn about twelve metres wide. Most would bring us 'goodies'. These had to be handed to the nurses and were all divided up. We each received an enamel plate with our afternoon tea on it, which consisted of a portion of pooled goodies. There were a few 'state children' who resided in Children's Homes and of course they had no visitors. I think the state children were what are now referred to as foster children. People would take them into their homes, for which the Government paid them a small sum. Most were treated well, but some were obtained to become servants.

When the parents left the hospital there was a real howling match, the parents also weeping and being very miserable. However, by the time they reached the exit gates the twenty beds had been carried back to the ward by the cheerful wardsmen and a sing-song commenced. As a young child I was always ill and it was thought I would never live to any age. One of the stories told was that when I was at the age of nearly two, my grandmother sat up late sewing a shroud for me when I was gravely ill with meningitis. (I suppose I wore it as a nightdress when I didn't die.)

Again, when I was seven, both my sister Dorothy and I were taken to the Coast Hospital with diphtheria. Whilst there we contracted scarlet fever and had to have our hair cut off. (Girls didn't have their hair cut short in 1911.) This time I nearly passed out with heart trouble and my parents, knocked up at 2 a.m. by a policeman, made the 10-mile journey post-haste in a hansom cab. It must have taken nearly all the family's savings to pay for it. However, for the second time I made it.

The family concluded that it must be unhealthy where we lived and decided to move house. So we moved to Newtown, but to a cottage no larger. It still had only three bedrooms, one for grandma and single daughter, one for the single son and the remaining one for my parents and we two girls, aged seven and nine years. It was a semi-detached cottage with a long passage. Off the kitchen was a little room with no window and a *stone* bath with a cold water tap over it. Hot water had to be carried in from the wash-house where it was heated in a bricked-in copper with a fire under it. We had to sit on a towel in the bath so our bottoms wouldn't get scratched. Mostly we were bathed in a big galvanised tub before the kitchen fire which was much more comfortable.

My sister was sent to a new school while I was still in hospital. Nearing the end of the school year the pupils were asked to bring some money for the prizes. My father who worked in the boot trade usually lost several weeks work, with of course no pay, about this time of the year so my mother couldn't give my sister any money. The children who didn't bring any were exhibited in front of the class by being made to stand on a 'form' (bench). Taking strong exception to this my mother immediately complained at the school and took my sister away from it.

We mostly wore dark coloured clothing to school but we always had white madapollam or calico drawers. These had embroidery round the legs, and we always wore white starched pinnies (pinafores) over our dresses. My mother used to make us lovely pinnies with an embroidery insertion down the front and embroidery lace on the bottom and sleeves. For Sundays we had hailstone muslin dresses with a blue or pink ribbon sash. We also had white hats that had the crown buttoned on to the rim by pearl buttons: sometimes with a couple of frills on the rim. The hats, too, were stiffly starched and threaded with ribbon the same colour as our sashes. We had hair ribbons to match, white shoes and three-quarter length white socks. Mother ironed all these garments with flat irons heated on the fire stove.

Our social life was connected with the church. We attended the Newtown Methodist. We had morning and afternoon Sunday school and there were always practices for the Sunday school anniversary. Crowded on these occasions, the church had a tiered platform erected at the front from which the children sang. Then there was the Sunday school concert with its many practices. My mother made us lovely costumes for these from 'cast-offs'.

On the first Saturday in November came the Sunday

10

school picnic. What a time we had! A special train took us to Parramatta Park or maybe a special tram to some other place. There were races, games and, when we were older, rowing on the river.

After the war ended in 1918 the world was swept by a dreadful calamity — the Influenza Pandemic. It is estimated that the total number of deaths was 21,640,000 all over the world. It started in France and practically no country escaped. Although Australia was then so isolated, it was swept with it. Germs were probably carried by the soldiers returning from the war. People died more quickly than coffins could be made for them. All public gatherings ceased — theatres, schools, churches, etc. Everyone had to wear a gauze mask over mouth and nose, and had to use an inhaler of some kind of steam disinfectant. These inhalers were installed in every work place. Church services were held in the open air: ours in Victoria Park next to Sydney University which we thought great fun.

Our next 'improved' move was directly across the street — a terrace house, again with only three bedrooms. We two girls had for our room the balcony outside our parents' room with a blind that rattled and bumped in bad weather. Though Dorothy and I did well at school we had no privacy for study. Our homework had to be done at the kitchen table and there were many distractions. When I was nearly fifteen I sat for and gained a half-scholarship to Stott's Business College and learned Pitman's shorthand, typing and bookkeeping. Then I worked in a Patent Attorney's office in Martin Place until I married in 1927. I was the only girl employed, doing everything necessary — typing, bookkeeping, filing, banking, receptionist, and occasionally even a little searching. I started at £1 per week, which was considered good money for a girl and gave my mother all my money from which she gave me back my fares and a little pocket money. She bought all my clothes, or made most of them.

Next door to us lived a very interesting, feckless family consisting of Mum, Dad and eight children. The father was a cabbie — hiring a hansom cab from the livery stables and

sitting on the cab rank at Newtown Bridge all day waiting for 'fares'. The mother was a hard-working little woman and when times were bad she used to go out washing. However, she wasn't very fond of cooking apparently. We could hear their conversation, being so close, and the usual routine was — 'Maudie, what do you want for your dinner?' 'I'll have a meat pie and a bottle of lemonade,' Maudie would say. The next one would want a saveloy and an iced cake, another fish and chips, and so on down the line. My grandma used to say, 'She ought to cook them a decent meal.' However, the funny thing was that these kids didn't seem to get sick and we did.

The WC or 'closet' as it was called (and sometimes something else) was at the end corner of the yard and my only solitude. I would sit there for ever so long singing, and it got the nickname of 'Ethel's Music Hall'. One of my favourite songs was 'Please give me a penny, sir, a penny please for bread . . .' and occasionally a penny would be thrown on the roof, which was quickly retrieved.

My father was a 'maker' in the boot trade, one uncle was a 'clicker' and someone else a 'sock and sizer'. Bootmakers were called 'snobs'. My father was an amateur song and dance comedian and often in demand for benefit nights. With no social services then, when a workmate was ill or his family in financial trouble a benefit concert would be arranged. They were something like the old time music hall, or might be half concert and half dance. Dad also at one time started a vaudeville show of his own but it was not very successful. I still have one of the programmes dated 1916: popular prices 6d and 1s.

Our errands to the cake, biscuit and pickle factories were not always done with good grace. We would get 6d worth of stale cakes from Miss Bishop's factory, a large brown paper bag full — sponges, chocolate, etc. — often eating the best before we got home. The same with broken biscuits from the biscuit factory: 'lolly' (iced) biscuits were a field day.

Three penn'orth of mixed pickles in a billycan we did not sample. The girl there who served us had yellow arms and hands and was always called 'Goldie'. If we were playing up, Dad used to threaten to send us to work at the pickle factory where we'd end up like Goldie.

Summer holidays were the brightest spot in our childhood but could not have been bright financially for my parents. My father would get the sack just before Christmas and the employees were told to watch the newspapers for the reopening date when they could return to work. Often this would mean several weeks without pay. We were never taken to the shops to see Father Christmas because we couldn't expect much in the way of presents. But my mother always saw that we got something in our socks. She was clever at making dolls' beds out of cardboard boxes and lovely dolls' clothes. She would save up all year to pay the rent for a furnished cottage at Freshwater, near Manly, for four or five weeks. It was 10s weekly.

It consisted of a little wooden, unlined structure of a living-kitchen-bedroom and another little bedroom. There was a deal table, two forms, a fire stove, four canvas stretchers (camp beds) and the very basic needs in pots and pans and a

little crockery. There may have been a few blankets and a tin dish to wash up in. We had candles for lighting and a tap came into the kitchen from an outside tank with a kerosene tin under the tap. We had to take everything else. We didn't need to take too many clothes however as we practically lived in our 'cossies' (bathers).

A ten-minute walk to the tram from home, half an hour tram ride to Circular Quay where we caught the Manly ferry, a short tram ride from Manly, then a trek over a big hill and by the time we reached our little wooden hut we were all very very tired. Tired or not, my mother had to prepare a meal, and we wanted to go to the beach.

This cottage was one of five built in a compound, with a community block consisting of a cold shower each for 'him' and 'her' and a pan toilet for each. The nightman used to collect the full pans during the day. He was a little bandy man, and we children used to issue a chorus of 'Pooh!' when we saw him approaching. He would retort with, 'Don't you be cheeky, there's plenty of yours in there'.

It was wonderful to be a family on our own. Our grandma, aunt and uncle didn't come except for a day visit. Dorothy and I were used to living with five adults, and though they were all very good to us, we had always to be careful not to do anything (at least in the open) of which they would disapprove. We had no privacy. It was particularly hard later

14

on when we had boy friends. Young people do not like to show their feelings to everyone. It's sometimes hard enough when it's just parents, but when it comes to aunt, uncle and grandma in addition, it's very difficult. Young people nowadays are much less inhibited than in my youth, but I think, nevertheless, there are times when they want to be alone.

The main streets during my young days were made out of wooden blocks, red gum I think. They were tarred over and a steam roller would compress the tar. A man carrying a red flag walked in front. In wet weather these blocks would get slippery and it was common to see a baker's or milkman's horse fallen over. Usually no damage was done to the animal but often the contents of the cart scattered over the road.

There were many street vendors. The prop man would come along the back lanes calling 'Clothes props, clothes props'; they were long branches of a tree with a fork at the top on which to raise the clothes line. They were about 9*d*. Then there was the rabbit man with his 'Rabbit-oh, rabbit-oh'. 'They're big today, lady.' And the organ-grinder and the tinker.

The milkman called twice a day and measured the milk into your billycan or jug from a big milk can. We even had a dairy in our street with live cows. We used to like going there: the lady would often give us a piece of frozen milk. Without refrigeration, I don't know how it was frozen. Also, I can't imagine where the cows grazed. Perhaps they were only hand fed. The yard was always a mess. When we had a halfpenny to spend we would buy a ha'porth of milk for ourselves as we didn't have milk as the usual thing. We always had a cup of tea from an early age.

In the back lane and front street we played hidey with our friends, and hopscotch, ball games and marbles. There were hardly any cars about. During the school holidays we were allowed to go to Camperdown Park, a mile walk away. There were swings here, and games going on that we could watch. The railway line wasn't far away and we would sometimes go down to watch the trains (steam trains of course). I remember when King Edward VII died, the trains all had purple and black drapings on the front of the engine.

In our street was the Coronation Hall owned by the Presbyterian Church, and they held in it an annual bazaar. This was a very big affair. Stalls were erected in the hall and decorated with coloured paper and flowers, and lots of goods were for sale: produce, home-made sweets, cakes: and a jumble stall full of knick-knackery. There were many competitions such as polishing a penny in the shortest time and men trimming a lady's hat. I once won a prize in the Best Dressed Doll competition, for which I received a trinket box.

I was married in 1927, the year Canberra became the seat of Federal Government. The Great Depression had begun but I was young, in love and looking forward to a rosy future. The menfolk in my family were out of work from time to time and I think I had accepted that this was a way of life.

We started off very modestly with a small weatherboard and fibro cottage at Sans Souci (NSW) where land was cheap at the time and with a bank loan of 6 per cent interest we were able to keep up our payments and didn't lose our home. Some of our friends who were more ambitious with their homes lost them.

My father lost his job and went on relief work digging sand at Botany. The work was too hard for him and he died at only forty-five years of age. My mother took in sewing and also did some housework. A very independent person, she wouldn't take help from us except indirectly. Only in her forties, she didn't qualify for a widow's pension, if there was one then. You were supposed to get work — but there was practically none to get.

My single uncle who lived in the family home was unemployed. He used to go to the bottle yards, collect bottles and jars which he carried home and washed, then filled them with hair shampoo, brilliantine, shaving cream and the like which he made in his shed. Then he hawked them from door to door. My husband used to help him make the preparations.

My grandmother was now able to get the old age pension and with the little my single aunt earned they were able to manage by pooling their resources. It was a terrible sight to see people evicted from their homes and the furniture being piled up on the footpath.

Some of the evicted people started up a 'squatting settlement' near La Perouse, on Botany Bay. It was called 'Happy Valley'. They built humpies from any old building material they could find, and they all helped each other. They were issued with food tickets to buy basic things and Chinese who ran vegetable gardens near by gave them vegetables they couldn't sell at the market. The Dairy Farmers Association donated 16 gallons of milk a day. Church organisations and private people helped with clothing, and my grandma used to make children's things from hand-me-downs, especially little boys' trousers. At least there was fresh clean air on the Bay then, not polluted like it is now.

At Coffs Harbour I had a relative who ran a banana plantation. When he sent down a consignment of bananas to Sydney, instead of receiving a cheque back he received an account for the ripening chamber. The price secured didn't even pay for the cartage. This made growers dump their produce, so while people were hungry, such a lot of food was wasted.

Our first child was a big, beautiful baby but very difficult and I, being very inexperienced, had to give over most of my time caring for her. I used to go and visit my mother and grandmother each week. I had a walk of 20 minutes from home to where I caught a steam tram to Kogarah railway station. Then I had to walk up a big flight of steps and down the other side to the platform where I caught the train to Erskineville. At Erskineville I had another steep flight of steps to walk up and then 15 minutes' walk to their home. I had to carry the heavy baby and all the necessary accessories so by the time I repeated the journey home I was very tired.

At the end of 1932 my husband was offered a position in Melbourne. We must have thought the Depression was over to have burnt our boats in taking it. How wrong we were!

In an old T-model Ford we left Sydney on Christmas Day 1932. (This car cost £15 and petrol was 1s 6d a gallon.) I didn't really want to go, and leave my family and friends, but I knew it was my duty to do so. I can still see my mother waving goodbye at the gate as we drove off. I cried when we left our home. But we arrived in Melbourne with only a few mishaps. Our second little girl was just getting over measles and I had to nurse her all the way. We rented a house for £1 a week but missed the beach where the children had so much fun. Then we bought land at Seaholme: then a quiet little rural village, no oil companies near by: and eventually had another home built.

My first friend was a lady whose husband was unemployed. They had six children. She had two sisters living in the country who would send her vegetables. She said that often they just pretended they had meat. Her husband had built a hall next door to their own little house. The Education Department rented this for school children too young to walk to the nearest school, Altona about 1½ miles away. The Methodist Church used it for a service on Sundays, and during the week a dance would be held in it. Admission price was 6d or 1s and we women would take a plate of refreshments. We also paid a small fee to the pianist who was glad of the money.

A number of men used to work on the roads. You would hear children singing in the street:

> You're on the susso now,
> You can't afford a cow;
> You live in a tent,
> You pay no rent,
> You're on the susso now.

There was no nastiness at Seaholme school but at Altona it must have been very difficult for children whose fathers were unemployed. These children were unable to buy their school books so they were on the 'free list'. These books were distinct from the bought ones in so far as they had red covers. The children must have felt this distinction with embarrassment. Shoes, also, were issued from time to time.

Lots of people lost everything in the Depression, but some made a lot of money. Houses could be bought very cheaply and those with money bought them, and other things, at bedrock prices, to resell at high prices when things looked up. Even people who retained their jobs lost something, too: their spirit of adventure. They would risk nothing for their security. Until the outbreak of the Second World War there were few jobs to be had, but when war broke out money came in millions for war equipment. Enlisting in the services was the first job some young people had since leaving school.

I suppose what made my life worth living then was that I had a good husband, a family I adored, and faith that things would turn out well in the end. But I'm sure that people who lost everything would have had a different outlook.

What is my life now? Well, I am very happy, or perhaps I should say contented, for how can one be completely happy when there is so much sorrow, sadness and uncertainty in our beautiful world?

Fortunately I am in good health. I think the illnesses I had in childhood have made me immune to many illnesses in later life. I can look back on a life well spent, I think, though there are many things that I would have done differently had I the experience I now have.

My husband and I are blessed with a marvellous family — two daughters and a son, all married and each have two children.

Naturally, if we had our time over, most of us would do something different to what we did in earlier life, in the way of education, but this was limited by economic conditions. In my case it was training to

earn my own living as early as possible. However, what I missed for myself I managed to achieve for my children. But one cannot live through one's children's lives, and when they have flown the nest one can feel empty and unfulfilled. This is where outside activity comes in.

I have always done a lot of voluntary work and have also attended classes at the Council of Adult Education. At present I am active in Pocket Theatre, a club of women who learn to act in small plays and perform them at church functions, various clubs and Senior Citizens' groups. I am also on the council of the Folklore Society, and a regular attendant and participant at their monthly gatherings. We also regularly attend the Templestowe & Doncaster Historical Society monthly meetings. Recently I organised a party for my husband's eightieth birthday. It was held in a local church hall and we had 130 guests, all friends and neighbours. It took the form of an old-fashioned party with items — singing and instrumental, a short play and dancing. Everyone voted it was the best party they had been to for years.

I recently read in a magazine an article by a woman in her eighties. She ends up with what I have taken as my motto:

'Never give up doing things because you are getting old.
You only get old because you give up doing things.'

Edna

Edna Denmead b.1906

I was born the youngest of seven children; we lived on a small rented farm near Drysdale, Victoria. We had two cows, in milk at different times, which provided butter and cheese and the skim milk left over fattened the pig. When the pig was killed Mother would daily rub into it saltpetre and brown sugar to preserve it. Then it would hang from the kitchen roof and provide the breakfast bacon.

We kept poultry and ducks and had eggs and birds for the table. Catching fish and rabbits were my brothers' jobs. Apples, pears, quinces, plums, etc. became jams and sauces. We buried swedes and carrots in sand to keep them through the winter and dug our own potatoes. Cauliflowers, cabbage and turnips we marketed in Geelong and we had a walk-in pantry always full of home-made goodies. We also made candles from mutton fat, floor and boot polish from beeswax after the honey had been drained, and needed to buy only things like flour (150 lb bags), sugar (70 lbs), tea (56 lb chests) and kerosene in cases (two 4-gallon tins per case) twice a year from Hoopers store in Geelong. Split in two, the tins were put in a frame for washing up dishes; or used whole to store jam in.

My grandmother became an invalid at an early age and my mother, as the eldest girl, had to take over the care of her and the seven other children. When she married my father at twenty-two years of age the doctor said she had worn herself out. She also had impaired sight from measles. As the youngest child I can't remember my mother ever able to work.

But my father was a very good man and my mother was always queen of the house. He got up while it was still dark, lit the fire and made tea and brought it to Mother and us girls in bed. The boys got up, had theirs, then went after the cows. My father always spent time with the axe to warm up and cut the day's firewood. The girls then got up and prepared breakfast which did not start until everyone was seated. It began with grace and ended in prayer for our safekeeping through the day.

My father earned money by seasonal work and selling vegetables, and Mother got a little from the sale of butter and eggs. They always tithed and gave a tenth of any earnings to the church. We children never saw or handled any money and barter was a way of life. A half side of a sheep killed by a neighbour would be paid for in kind, whatever the neighbour lacked, like potatoes. Even the doctor, driving out from Geelong, would return with his buggy piled with produce after spending the night till a crisis had passed — no doubt he gave most of it to poor patients in the city.

My mother insisted on a well-run home.

Monday: Washday. Clothes were sorted, soaked, hand washed, boiled, rinsed twice, blued and starched.

Tuesday: Ironing.

Wednesday and Thursday: Cleaning of bedrooms.

Friday: Dining room and kitchen were made spotless for Sunday. The kitchen table, the dresser and the form for seating were made of white wood and sandsoap and elbow grease was needed in large amounts to keep them white. The stove was black-leaded and the dining room fireplace white-washed.

Saturday: The big day. Set the sponge for the week's supply of bread. Yeast was made from potato water, sugar, and a little of the last bottle of yeast. After breakfast the sponge was kneaded and flour added, then covered up warm and put in front of the fire to rise. Shin of beef, bacon bones and scraps cooked for several hours became bowls of potted meat. Meat for Sunday was roasted, and buns, cream puffs and Victoria sandwich were baked, as no work was done on Sunday except baking potatoes in their jackets.

Sunday: A fine black horse called Pompey pulled us in the wagonette to church. He was always reluctant to start off till Father gave a cut with the whip, then he would set off at breakneck speed. I think perhaps this is where I learned to enjoy living dangerously.

In 1913, after my grandfather left some money to Mother, my parents bought a house with an acre of land in the Western District. Life continued much the same but we had only one cow. My father got work with the Shire Council, patrolling and maintaining the roads, and did not retire until he was seventy-three years old — when they could no longer insure him. He was a goodlooking man who, even till he died at eighty-seven, had an upright carriage.

There were never any quarrels allowed with us children. My mother would open the door and say, 'We will let the bad spirit pass out,' and we would stand in awe expecting to see it do so. If my father and mother had differences it was behind closed doors. We never saw any. Mother administered our punishment, my father never hit one of us.

Mother was excellent with home remedies. Saturdays we were lined up and had to drink a cup of senna tea. I always played up and had to have my nose held. In the spring it was nettle tea for spots, also sulphur and treacle. I grew up skinny, tough and healthy. My second sister was delicate and died at forty-five. The rest of us have made our seventies. My eldest sister lived till ninety and a brother and sister still living are in their eighties.

My brother is in New South Wales, my sister in South Australia. 'Don't quarrel, children, you will scatter to the four winds,' I hear my mother say.

At fourteen, after getting my Merit certificate, I left school to take over the care of my invalid mother, the eight-roomed house, etc., while my elder sister, aged nineteen, was able to go out to work and earn money to put her through the Salvation Army College and become an officer.

I loved my mother and it was no burden to care for her though her illness (dropsy) had made her a very big person and I was only 6½ stone. Apart from the housework every morning I would have to sponge and dress her. Her corsets and boots had to be made to order. Each night she liked me to brush and plait her hair, bathe her feet and read to her. Now I wonder how I ever managed everything, baking bread and making butter as well. It was then I began to write stories and poems and the first money I ever earned was at fifteen when I was asked to report the weekly doings for the *Geelong News of the Week*.

When I was sixteen an older sister decided to come home and my mother passed away shortly afterwards.

'Never spend the last until the next is in your hand,' my mother used to say. I had been married seven years when we first felt the impact of no money. My husband, when he lost his job at the butter factory, was not equipped to battle. He

had been at school till he was eighteen and in those days you were only taught to be a gentleman.

I had two small children and we were buying our home; we had a good vegetable garden, poultry and two ferrets. Three days a week my husband would ride off on his bicycle with ferrets and nets, returning with all he could carry on the handlebars. We then had to skin and peg out the skins and I would wash and prepare the good carcasses for sale next day. A pair of rabbits brought sixpence when hawked from door to door. Two pounds of rabbit skins would buy a week's groceries. They were in demand for export to Italy where the fur was used to make men's hats. Sometimes we could exchange a pair of rabbits for fresh-caught fish. My neighbour had a cow and she gave me a billy of milk daily. In return I cut down clothes and made dresses for her six children.

In those days the baker and butcher called. Threepence for a pound of lamb, and a shilling for a forequarter. We bought when we had money and if we had none the baker would always have a stale loaf to give. The butcher would give you soup bones, liver, brains, etc., if you were a genuine battler.

I made all my children's clothes and they never looked poor. We always had a meal before us. Shoes were a problem. My eldest girl started school and came home wet-footed. I found money to buy a new pair of boots. Next day she came home wet halfway up her legs. The boy nextdoor had walked home in the gutter, and she had done the same.

The Government started Relief Works down in the Otways and Rail Work up Cressy way. It had been a great comedown for my husband to accept 'susso' (sustenance pay) but among others he offered to work from 1 o'clock till 4 o'clock for two days a week in the Public Gardens in return.

We had to move out of the home we were buying because we couldn't keep up the payments. There were many empty houses to choose from. Some owners would even allow free rent to a good tenant to save them from vandalism by squatters. I managed to get a job at a restaurant working 10 a.m. till 8 p.m. daily and a half day Saturday. The wages were £2 weekly. But I could take food left over at night home to the family. Then my employer decided to close. Talking things over, I agreed to work for £1 a week, signing for the £2. Half a loaf was better than none and there were more left-over meals each day to take home.

Edna with daughters

26

Looking back on those years when a penny had to do the work of a shilling I think one got more pleasure out of spending money. It certainly made one careful for life.

I have always loved nature and for the past twenty-odd years I have fulfilled my lifelong desire to travel. There are few places in Australia I have not been and I even managed to take three of my grandchildren on the flight to Antarctica.

As a member of a Gem and Mineral Club for ten years I visited most of the five opal fields more than once and also sapphire fields, petrified wood and palm and many other semi-precious gem fields.

Growing old means a long hard climb through life's many experiences, both good and bad. We look back on the panorama of our life. But it isn't all looking back. Having a family is the biggest plus. I have three daughters, all married, eight grandchildren and eight great grandchildren. Where there are four generations, life is never boring as each member contributes to life's pattern, some more, some less.

There are so many opportunities available in clubs, travel, adult learning classes; I chose Australian History, Creative Writing, Woodwork and Gemology. It doesn't really matter what you choose so long as you keep learning.

After the successful treatment of my illness I joined the Geelong Cancer After-care Group which one woman initiated. It's aim is to give support to those who have had surgery or other treatment for cancer. We meet together twice a month. Visits, cards, flowers and outings, plus home phone calls, all help to say, 'We are thinking of you'. And we have raised money to help establish an Oncology department at the Geelong Hospital, which saves many people from having to travel to Melbourne for treatment. Working with the group has given a new purpose to my life and I am truly grateful for all my friends here.

I think the greatest blessing when one grows old, is to love and be loved. The Bible says, 'Love your neighbour as yourself that your days may be long upon the earth.'

Those of us who are now in the autumn of our lives can be grateful for our early Christian upbringing. How comforting it was when we were small children that a prayer was offered before we left home in the morning for our safekeeping through the day, and again when we made ready for our bed at night. And now there is still the comfort of one's chosen church and the love and support of its members, believing that when your life comes to a close God waits to take your hand, forgiving the mistakes, rewarding any good you have done.

Stella

Stella Garvey b.1906

ON 30 September 1906 Emilie Hogan excused herself from a game of cards and shortly afterwards gave birth to a premature girl-child who was christened Stella Margaret (Margaret after her dear friend Maggie Lloyd — sister of Ned Kelly). Three years later my sister Loretta (Lol) was born, my loving generous friend all her days. Those years in the bush at Greta (Victoria) remain dim in memory. We moved to Benalla when I was three. But I can recall a hot summer's night in front of our place and children dragging me up and down in a hessian bag, joyously bounded about by a dog; and my older sisters Mary, Kathleen and Lou bringing back the washing from the creek.

In Benalla, at the fringe of town, our house stood on nearly an acre. Dad planted fruit trees and vegetables and kept a few fowls. A huge mulberry tree overhung a separate kitchen, a source of luscious fruit and our refuge in times of trouble. There we were safe from our mother when she was on the warpath. There we read the forbidden books. A story, 'Mary Latimer, Nun', absolutely thrilled me. But in the old kitchen, rarely used, we played dress-ups with our friends and enacted plays which Lol and I wrote.

Measles meant, then, three weeks away from school. When two of our friends got measles we had them breathe over us; it worked and we too soon had measles. I never liked

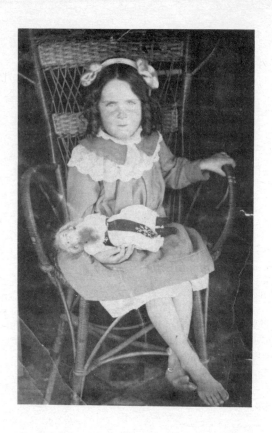

school and often had strange pains in the stomach which,
when I was kept home, disappeared once the school bell
rang.

   We caught yabbies from a nearby waterhole with a lump
of meat on a piece of cotton and a colander to dip under
when it tightened signalling a catch. There was a square of
green couch grass there that we called 'our lawn' where we
picnicked. And in the surrounding paddocks I'd dreamily
wander with my bucket looking for mushrooms. Once I
found a patch of wild violets; it was a glimpse of
fairyland.

   Dad was a carpenter and builder, always in work as he
was a good tradesman. But he was no businessman, people
were often slow to pay so there was always a dire shortage of
ready cash.

We wore heavy lace-up boots to school (shoes were for Sunday) and had a school dress each and one best one each for Sunday. Mum's pride was that we looked as good as the best of them when we went out. So our hair was washed and brushed and polished with a silk handkerchief and nearly every evening a fine toothcomb dipped in kerosene was combed through it to keep nits and lice at bay. The night before the local show our hair was done up in 'rags' — strips of cloth wound round strands of hair and when taken off next day we had an array of sausage curls.

For our first Communion Mum managed to buy two cream silk handworked dresses imported from Genoa. I can still see and feel the lovely soft silk. Mum must have done without a few things to purchase those. Dear Mum, she was generous and loving even though hot-tempered and a firm disciplinarian. As I get older I understand my parents more. We are apt to blame them for our own weaknesses; it takes a long time and much experience to realise our responsibility for our own conduct.

I think I just stoically endured school between holidays, usually spent with my dear friends the Lloyd family in Greta. Tom Lloyd (father) was a cousin of Ned Kelly and he made the armour which Ned used, from flattened ploughshares. Mrs Lloyd (Rachael) was a sister of Steve Hart. Dorrie, Tin, Tom and Leo were all round about my age. Just before holidays a letter would arrive — 'Be sure and come, we will meet you at Glenrowan with the ponies.' I would take the train to Glenrowan and then the six or seven miles per pony to Greta. We roamed the bush, bathing in the little creek that ran through their property. The boys often played jokes on me; they thought I was a city slicker, coming as I did from what to them was almost a city.

At home in Benalla our household equipment was spare. A few hooks fastened to the corner of a wall for our clothes and a curtain strung across sufficed for a wardrobe. We had lino in the sitting room which we called the 'front room' and two lovely pieces of furniture from our grandmother's — a cedar chest of drawers and cedar oval table. We had plenty of good books of poetry and a number of the classics. There was an open fireplace in the front room and a wood-burning stove in the kitchen which was kept glossy with black lead. There were candles and kerosene lamps for lighting and Lol and I collected bark each evening for the morning fire.

On washing day the clothes were washed in a tub on a bench outside near the tap and then boiled in a kerosene tin over a fire in the brick fireplace. It must have been backbreaking work bending and lifting from tub to fireplace. My mother's hands were all criss-crossed with dark cracks from scrubbing and washing. With only soap, washing soda and blue, the washing was always brought in white and sweetsmelling from the line.

We had the usual Coolgardie safe* and cooking utensils were all black cast-iron. We only used our bath in summer; in winter we bathed once a week in a tub in front of the kitchen fire.

Mum was a midwife whose bag was always packed with her large white starched apron and cap and her toilet requisites. Dad was a good Catholic but Mum was brought up Church of England, so we had a foot in both camps. We ate meat on Fridays, never kept the Saints' days and often missed Mass. I had a strong religious bent and prayed to be given the miracle of faith the priest preached about but somehow it eluded me. I felt guilty about this for many years and only when I gave away all orthodox belief did I discover a faith that came slowly after so much doubt; there are still doubts but faith remains. I think it is a faith that I must always hold to help me search for the good in myself and all others in my contact. There is no end to this: as I advance one step there is another one ahead. I find it an exciting journey.

My mother married at nineteen and Dad was thirty-nine. The marriage was arranged by her brother-in-law. Mum wasn't in love; she told me she thought only of the wedding and dressing as a bride. Dad loved Mum all his days. He told me once that none of us was as pretty as our mother. I know

---

*Coolgardie safe: made of flywire covered with hessian. A galvanised-tin top held about two gallons (9.1 litres) of water which, with the aid of strips of flannel or towelling, ran down the sides of the safe keeping the hessian wet. A galvanised-tin guttering at the bottom ran the water into a bucket.

that Mum fell deeply in love later, but in those days marriage was for keeps so their marriage endured. Mum nursed Dad lovingly right to the end when he died of tuberculosis at the age of seventy-six.

Mum's father was a Cambridge graduate, a son of a Church of England clergyman but disowned by his family. It seems he wrote for *Steads* and *Cornhill* magazines. My mother was country correspondent for the *Bulletin* and also Registrar of Births and Deaths, which supplemented the family finances. Her own mother was born in Cork, Ireland.

Dad was adopted by a farmer and his wife. His Irish parents and their large family went off to the goldfields and he never saw or heard of them again. I never remember Dad being other than gentle and kind. They always made the most of what joy came their way. We had lots of visitors for social evenings. Mum would attend a concert to hear a visiting singer of renown. She was an active member of the Labor Party and a fervent anti-conscriptionist in 1916–17. World events were discussed at home, especially the Irish Question.

I was about eight when the First World War broke out. The papers were full of the dreadful atrocities done by the Germans; we believed it all. In 1915 when my brother Cec was sixteen he announced that he was enlisting and needed Mum's permission. When she refused he said he would run away and enlist. So she agreed reluctantly and he put his age up to eighteen and was accepted.

He was an idealistic youth who loved poetry, literature and all worthwhile things. He was then still at high school working part time at a newsagency to pay his way. Each pay day he would bring a present for the kidlets, as he called Lol and me. When told of his decision his headmaster said, 'It was as if at the beach he had picked up a handful of sand which held a pearl, when suddenly the waves washed it away.'

Cec was on the *Southland* when it was torpedoed on the way to Gallipoli. After Gallipoli came the mud and blood of the dreadful Somme. I now feel most of the men who went to fight were not moved by love of a scrap, but from a desire to help save the world from evil. Many, like Cec, had never been away from home before and were quite innocent in the ways of the world.

On 11 November when the war ended, Lol and I rushed up the main street in our nightgowns. People everywhere were dancing and singing, wild with delight. The war was over, sons, husbands, lovers and brothers would return — well, the survivors would.

There was a great welcome for Cec. Dad festooned the verandah with garlands of greenery and streamers and a big 'Welcome Home' sign. Lashings of food were served in our big kitchen: laughing, crying friends were dropping in to shake Cec's hand; the family was in a euphoria of joy, our brother safely home at last.

Cec came home, yes, but the war had played havoc with my dear brother. He drank heavily till he died of TB at the age of fifty-two. His death was a bitter grief to me. So much promise of a truly loving human being, his full potential unrealised because of a foul war.

But it was wonderful to have my beloved brother home at last. He was, unfortunately, most critical of the books we were reading and our behaviour in general. Lol and I were romantic and loved to read True Life Romances and other trashy publications; Cec certainly disapproved of those.

Another memory of 1918 is my being in love with Jack C. We were determined to marry when we grew up. It was a childish affair, apart from a chaste kiss or two: but the joy was just as intense as adult love experienced later. I can still remember the thrill of waiting at our gate for Jack, who sometimes brought me a bunch of wildflowers and apple blossom.

Sexual education was non-existent then. I once asked a friend at school if she was going swimming that day. She answered importantly, 'Oh no, I'm not well.' I laughed, thinking she was joking as she looked very well indeed. She then told me she had her monthly period. That evening I asked Mum and she explained what it meant. But mine didn't arrive till I was sixteen so I didn't have to worry about it at school.

34

At about thirteen I went to live with my sister Kath, her husband and little girl. Dad had TB and Mum was finding it hard to make ends meet. I went from Newport to Williamstown High School by train but sometimes walked home to save the fare for pocket money. The girls seemed mostly a well-dressed lot and had nice polished leather suitcases, but my suitcase was a monstrous cane affair. God knows how many of my older relatives had used it. It was a genuine antique in which my books rattled around like pebbles. I could have fitted myself in it quite easily. My overcoat was also inherited. It was like a piece of woollen sculpture, so solid it could stand up on its own. Oh, how I hated that case and coat. Then, lucky lucky me! My loving and kind sister bought me a complete school outfit. At last I was dressed like the rest of the girls.

One teacher I shall never forget was a Mr Geraghty, a large rather eccentric man who gave the boys a terrible time but thought the girls little angels. I quickly realised I could get away with very little work and many mistakes just by looking helpless. 'I couldn't manage the algebra, sir.' 'Never mind my dear, you did your best.'

My term report book with its record of low marks was a problem. I was afraid to show it to Mum, so always willing to take a chance I altered the marks and kept harmony in the home. Then the returned report had to have the alterations erased. I don't know how this skulduggery was never detected. I was fourteen when I finished my third year at high school and returned to Benalla to get a job.

My first job was looking after two little children for 8s a week and live at home. I was also supposed to help with the housework: a large wooden-floored return verandah to be scrubbed on hands and knees, a bedroom to be dusted and its floor polished each day and a hall likewise. Then the kitchen floor had to be washed, the black iron wood-burning stove black-leaded and the surrounding bricks whitewashed. After that I took the children for a walk accompanied by their female dog which when on heat was a terrible embarrassment to me.

The only thing I liked about the job was the food. Mrs C. was a good cook and made very tasty meals. Both husband

and wife were miserable and depressed people who never joked and rarely smiled, and sadly the children followed suit. I wasn't much good at housework as most of the time I was dreaming my dreams. While I was polishing the bedroom floor I would stop and sit in front of the large dressing-table mirror seeing myself as some beautiful heroine of romance. I even tried a dab of powder and perfume.

Our ways parted very soon. It was Saturday morning and Mrs C. complained about a spot of whitewash on the stove, and told me to do it again. That was just too much, I was already late for the football. My heated, 'I'm leaving and not coming back,' meant the end of my first job.

My next was at the Railway Refreshment Rooms as a counter attendant. There were about ten girls and one boy on the staff and we all lived in. The bedrooms on the floor above were comfortable, the food good and to my great pleasure there was plenty of hot water for baths and showers. It was an excellent environment for a young girl away from home as there was always lots of fun going on and plenty of friends to go out with.

The Railways Institute held dances, socials and other

The Railway Refreshment Room staff (Stella second left, back row)

activities. Fancy-dress balls were a favourite and there was
no shortage of dancing partners as we had our own group of
boys who escorted us and saw that we never missed a dance.
On summer evenings we would all go for a walk to the
Icecream Parlour or Tearooms in the main street where we
would live it up on sundaes, icecream sodas and soft drinks.
There was once a visit from Phillip Lytton's Theatrical
Company which performed 'East Lynne' in a large
marquee. We wept real tears over it and another wonderful
melodrama called 'Shot at the Altar'.

We often went on picnics; the boys hired the van and the
girls provided the food. Coming home at dusk, tired and
happy, we loved to sit on the back of the van with our legs
dangling and sing all the way home. Then when I was
eighteen my dear father died which altered my whole life. I
decided I wanted to move to Melbourne on my own. This
outraged Mum and she predicted all sorts of disasters likely
to befall me in the city. Nevertheless, I firmly packed my
bags and left. I first stayed with Uncle Harry and Aunt Lil
who never missed the Monday morning star bargain day at
Myers when she would come home with yet another useless
ornament to add to her already large collection. It must have
been quite a job dusting.

I eventually answered an ad. in the paper for a waitress at
Carlyon's hotel in Spencer Street. I must have looked the
typical country girl with my long black hair and clutching a
grey coat round my slight figure: my brown straw hat was
rather like a coal scuttle.

Did I know 'A la Carte' waiting? No, but I am quick to
learn. Madame must have thought so too.

Later on Mum and my sister Lol moved to Melbourne
which meant the heartbreaking task of house-hunting. The
meagre budget was so limiting. It was depressing finding our
way in a strange city to inspect houses that were so filthy and
rundown that they were impossible. The decent houses were
beyond our means. We would arrive back at Aunt Lil's tired
out and bad tempered with each other. Then Mum found a
freshly renovated brick cottage in a suitable street and within
walking distance of the station.

Lol got a job at a college in Parkville, so with two wage earners, plus a small sum my brother Cec sent Mum each week, we got by and were happy to be together again.

At Carlyon's the cavernous kitchen with the chef and his assistants rather intimidated me, and a large glowing charcoal fire for the grills made the kitchen look like Dante's Inferno. But I learnt to shout my orders loudly and was determined to be served when it came my turn.

Cec and his fiancee, Ellie, came to live with us. Ellie worked at Yarra Falls Woollen Mills and soon I joined her there. The noise of the huge weaving looms was just about intolerable, filling my head like the noise of a thousand cicadas. This din stayed in my head day and night for the first two weeks: after that I didn't notice it so much. The only way we could communicate with each other was by shouting which left me depleted at the end of the day. My stay was cut short by an attack of appendicitis and afterwards I worked as a waitress in a combined restaurant and home-made cake shop, became cashier and then manageress of the cake counter: I loved meeting and dealing with people from many walks of life.

Lol and I became night students at the National Gallery Art School: we didn't have any talent but lots of dreams. St Kilda Beach was a popular rendezvous on summer evenings and we would sit around with friends, someone with a guitar, and sing, talk, laugh and discuss seriously some of the problems of the world like why there should be wars, and poverty side by side with riches. We ardently embraced the socialistic ideas of American author, Upton Sinclair. The First World War must have had a profound effect on our thinking in those times.

We now live in a snug home on the banks of the River Plenty in the midst of a lovely, somewhat wild, bush garden. In my heart I call it 'Beulah', the promised land, because here I have found inner peace and strength that I hope is with me all my days.

Lots of people pass by our place close to the high curving bridge

across the river that connects us to the town and railway station: friendly people who wave a greeting to us as they pass by.

We have good neighbours and some have become our most treasured friends — their kindness at times overwhelms us. There are lots of young people, most we have known since they were born and rather like a big extended family. Young Paul, one of a family of twelve, once spent his pocket money, $1.50, to buy us a chocolate rooster for Easter. Brian, from another large family, brings the Herald each evening to save Jim a walk. He and his brother Peter see that we get a share of the fruit when in season.

Anna, thirteen, learning to cook, shares her baking with us. Damien, her older brother, wrote me a beautiful poem for my seventy-sixth birthday, and Julian, younger, wrote about me in an essay. These are precious memories to cherish.

Glen, studying for the ministry, called a few days ago and we talked for two hours, each searching for meaning and gaining spiritual strength from each other. There are many other old and young people whom I meet that give me faith in the future. I hope also that I give them hope. A special delight is when friends arrive unexpectedly and share a pot-luck meal.

Hardly a day passes without someone arriving, and each day brings its measure of fulfilment, whether I am potting plants for stalls or friends, cooking a big pot of soup to share with someone who lives alone, or doing my daily household chores. In a creative mood I make pressed flower cards for special occasions.

Our marriage has grown into a marvellously harmonious relationship after a few ups and downs during forty-odd years together. Like some wine it gets better with age. Our four married children and their families live not far away, which is a great boon, as they are most helpful and loving towards us.

I could go on and on — there are many small, lovely experiences that I cannot put into words, which add greatly to zest for my life. Finally I know that life is worth living for me in spite of all the hazards and I am finding it as rich and exciting at seventy-nine as I did at twenty-five.

Ellinor

Ellinor Buchanan b.1892

IN 1861, when my mother was two years old, her father Robert Duff was killed when thrown from his horse against a tree on the way home from Dandenong market. Annie Adelaide, her sister, was four. They were both born at Maxifield near Berwick, Victoria. Grandmother married again in 1866, Edward Tucker from Cranbourne, and he died only six years later.

My mother Emily Eva Duff and my father, Henry Clarke Sharp were married at my grandmother's home 'Fernlea' in Clyde (Victoria) in August 1889. My brother Harry was born a year later and I on 9 September 1892, my brother George in 1894. Of course I don't remember being born but my mother said I was in too much of a hurry and she wanted to wait for the midwife — so she crossed her legs.

The house we lived in was called 'Wilandra' after a station property in New South Wales where my father had been a jackeroo. Mother had a girl, Maggie Flynn, to help in the house. The Flynn girls were wonderful and two others came after Maggie. Then we had Mabel G. who got into mischief with one of the workmen. Mother locked the door at night but never dreamed the workman helped Mabel out of the window.

We had cows, probably Ayrshires, but not stud cattle, and

41

Harry, Ellinor, baby George and mother at Wilandra. Grandmother Tucker in phaeton drawn by Toby

we had a big cowshed with a race down the middle and about ten cowbails on either side. The fresh milk was taken each morning to Clyde railway station loaded on the spring cart. Perhaps it was called a 'spring cart' because it bounced over a rough road, but it certainly had no springs.

Harry could not have been more than ten years old when he was entrusted to drive the cart to the station where probably a porter unloaded it. It upset my mother in case Harry had to unload on his own. The milk had first to be cooled in a cooler: a big square arrangement of tin with serrations and tubes that had cold water in them. The milk ran over the tubes and was cooled.

Father worked hard at sowing time. The paddock was ploughed with a horse and single furrow plough and then Father strode the paddock with the seed in a bag on his chest, flinging handfuls of seed either side as he walked. Then the paddock was harrowed.

The summer of 1898 was the year of the dreadful fires in Gippsland. I was five and I sat on the steps of our home in the hot summer evening watching the fires burning. The whole of the Great Dividing Range seemed a ridge of flames in the night. Burning leaves were drawn up into the sky by the hot air currents and carried the fires for miles, and leaves of trees known to be growing no closer than sixty or seventy miles away were found afterwards. At Toora some of the children at school who had been told to wait for their parents became

Ellinor, George and Harry, about 1897

anxious and started off home along the bush track. Five were burned to death.

When I was five years old I had my first trip to Sydney with Mother, Harry and baby George. It was nearly my last. We were coming up Pitt Street in one of the horse-drawn double-decker buses — the buses were drawn by four horses — and Mother and Great-aunt alighted at Farmers' corner. Mother went across with George and I was left with Aunt Tilly while she paid the fare, but I ran across the road to join my mother, right in the path of an oncoming carriage and pair. A man grabbed me by the armpits and swung me to safety on the pavement, a second away from the horses' plunging hooves. The horses' heads were right above me.

I used to be taken to the Presbyterian church in Cranbourne, but not my brothers as it was a single-seated buggy and comfortable only for two adults and one child. It was four miles and it seemed to take a long time getting there as, sitting between my parents and being small, I didn't seem to get my share of air.

We all wore Sunday best for church, Father a stiff collar, white shirt and a suit fashionable for the day, and Mother's dress had a small bustle. Halfway we would meet our neighbours the Kennedys, returning from their Roman Catholic service, by which we knew we were on time. My

43

father would pull up our horse and would exchange news with the Kennedys. Then we drove on and were in nice time for our service.

We paid an annual rent for our pew, an ordinary wooden pew with a place for a name card to be slipped in at the end of it. At the back of the church were seats for those not paying rent. I didn't sit in a box pew until I went to Sydney: there the usher would conduct us to the pew and he would shut the door when we were inside and only the minister could see us.

I liked the hymns. I am fond of church music but I got very tired of prayers and the talking of the minister which I did not understand, so once I watched a louse crawl on the collar of the boy who sat in front and I thought, 'His older stepsister does not comb his hair with a fine tooth comb.' His mother had died when he was younger. My mother was careful with my brothers' hair and mine was plaited when I started school.

When church at last finished there was further talk with friends, then we drove a short distance to some elderly relatives where I sat in the buggy while my parents paid their visit. Then we drove home and I was glad to have a hot roast dinner. I was then allowed to read my favourite Sunday stories in the *Quiver* — very heavy reading for children and about the Fairchild family where children never seemed to do anything wrong or get into mischief. On wet Sundays Mother would read to us from *Sunday at Home*. I liked that very much. Even my brothers liked being read to.

Twice a year the Reverend Mr Rock visited us at home. He would be entertained with ceremony in the drawing room and before leaving he'd always say, 'We'll have a prayer'. I remember kneeling facing my chair for the prayer.

My pony was called Toby. He had a habit of biting and always went for a barbed wire fence or the boxthorn hedge and tried to scratch me. When I used to take him into the garden to eat grass he wouldn't start until he'd been to the apricot tree where I reached for an apricot, then he turned his head sideways while I lent forward to give it to him.

44

I rode to school on a pony called Dick with a white star on his forehead. He was inclined to open gates so had to be shut up in the churchyard by himself because if he was in the schoolyard he'd open gates and let all the ponies out. He was a very handy pony and willing to take short cuts. I'd climb over obstacles and, taking the reins, encourage him to jump. Before I went to school my brother Harry said to me, 'Yah, you can't go to school until you can canter!' so one day I took Dick out on the road and kicked him and kicked him until he eventually decided to break into a canter, with me hanging on round his neck.

I was eight when my grandmother Tucker died (Mother's mother). The clergyman had been visiting at 'Fernlea' and he and my grandmother were sitting there talking when suddenly she said, 'Oh, Annie!' (her elder child's name) and she died, sitting there. The clergyman came to tell Mother who was upset, and shortly he came out to where I was playing, with two half-crowns in his hand. He said, 'You take these over to your grandmother's. Knock — there is no need to go inside — and you are to say, "Put them on".' He repeated, 'You've no need to go inside,' but when I got there the housekeeper asked would I like to see my grandmother so I went and saw her lying there. The half-crowns were to keep her eyelids shut.

At Clyde our bread was delivered by horse-drawn baker's cart, and the butcher came in a cart affair the back of which let down to make a shelf for him to weigh the meat on. Our school lunches were bread and jam. The mail must have come by train and the schoolteacher gave out the letters to the children to take home. I remember the smell of the red sealing wax which the schoolmaster used to seal the mail bag which was to go away. That meant school was nearly out.

The failure of the Banks in Melbourne in the early 1890s brought poverty to quite a number of people, especially to single women depending on investments for their income. Mother always said that the Property Rights law came in just in time to save her. The new law passed meant that women could have money and possessions in their own right, but previously everything they owned or inherited became their husband's. Mother may have had a little money when Grandmother Tucker died, but she kept £100 each for our education. George wouldn't have cared if he'd never had another lesson in his life but when we moved to Sydney he was sent to the Workingman's College — the 'Tech' — so that he could learn to do things with his hands.

The railway line when it went through was very important to Gippsland. First it went to Korumburra and later the line was built to Welshpool: I think because Melbourne needed the fish. The railway lines had enabled the country to entertain Prince Alfred, a son of Queen Victoria, and his entourage. That was in 1867 but I remember being told about the train going through. I've an idea the prince may have been sent abroad to keep him out of mischief at home, but the history books don't say that.

I seem to have lived such very different kinds of lives — Clyde, Cranbourne, Flinders, Sydney, and this has been a little about Clyde where I was born: where we learned not to play under the clump of pampas grass or our fingers might get cut on the leaves, and where my mother gave us our first lessons round the table. George would disappear under the table.

Later, Clyde was where we went to school. I remember frosty days in winter with the water freezing to a thin sheet of ice on the shallow puddles, chilblains, and the ice frightening the ponies when their hooves cracked it.

When I was very young I always wore a pinafore over my dress and I had black stockings and buttoned boots. I usually rode astride but when we went to Flinders I had a side-saddle. There were no telephones, no wirelesses, no television, no cars and no aeroplanes. Queen Victoria's Diamond Jubilee was 22 June 1897, and the Boer War began in 1899. My elder brother Harry was always singing, 'Soldiers of the Queen' — the words were on the back of a penny surprise-packet of lollies. In 1901 we moved to Cardinia before going on to Flinders, so I went to five different schools in all — Clyde, Cardinia, Flinders, Cape Schanck (called Blacks' Camp) Flinders and Merton Hall.

So many incidents, anecdotes and characters have become family folklore now. There used to be a rather select wealthy family called the A'Becketts who visited sometimes. There was always a great flurry of tidying up and preparation as for illustrious guests, and so it became a saying over the years, when important guests were expected, 'The A'Becketts are coming'.

Mr Bill Singleton was a Flinders identity and I remember things about him, things he said, as if it were yesterday. We were living at 'Walmeryong', Flinders, and I must have been about twelve as I hadn't yet gone away to school.

The workmen had their table in the wash-house — a nice bright room with the copper at one end.

'Do you want any more?' Bill asked the fellow sitting next to him. The men were finishing their dinner. It was bread-and-butter pudding with plenty of nice eggs in it. The townie chap said, 'No thank you,' so Bill said, 'I'd better finish it then,' and took the whole lot.

I never saw Bill on a horse. He must have walked everywhere. While with us he lived in a room over in the shed. It had been a harness room. The extension which was the men's toilet was built on to the henhouse. Bill was a bachelor. He never seemed to think of marrying. He was having his meal one day when he said, 'Maggie's a good cook, isn't she? Do you think she'd marry me if I asked her? He! He! He!' he laughed to himself. It sounded deeper coming out of his chest than it would out of mine.

He was a workman who hadn't had much schooling: a good workman under orders. He liked to be told what to do. Walking past as Bill was still having his meal, my father said, 'When you've finished, Bill, knock up a bit of wood.'

'Knock up a bit of wood. He! He! He means, "Fill the wood box! Leave the barrow full!"' Bill wasn't as dumb as he looked.

Rabbits were very plentiful and he helped to dig out rabbit warrens at 'Clondrisse'. 'Clondrisse' was 5 miles out from Flinders on the Cape Schanck Road on a headland overlooking the ocean. The house was two-storey, an old building which had been added to and it had tall pine trees and cypresses round it as windbreaks. Cypresses make better windbreaks than pine trees as they are compact and don't catch the wind so much. A sheoak never grows tall and it is very good too, very like pine and not like an oak at all. There can be a lot of windy weather at Flinders.

'What did you have for dinner, Bill?' someone asked. 'I had rabbit for breakfast, I had rabbit for dinner and I had rabbit for tea. I've had so much rabbit I'm afraid to pass a dog on the way into Flinders.'

During the Depression Bill Singleton was killed on the Holland's property at Flinders. He would take piece-work anywhere, as long as it was heavy work, and he was killed under a tree he'd been cutting down with an axe. He'd crawled for a tool under the tree after it fell and a branch settled and crushed him. Mr Tom Holland had heard someone calling — he thought the sound was from boys walking along the cliffs — and it wasn't until it came to four or five o'clock when Bill would have been up at the house working for them (he was regular as clockwork) that Mr Holland became anxious and went to look for him.

You must never crawl under a fallen tree. It might look safe but vibration can shake the branches off balance, or the tree may still be settling.

I can remember the First World War better than the Second. And one day in 1917 when Mother and I were coming back from a lovely day in Sydney shopping, we saw the minister walking towards us. I know we'd had lunch at Mark Foys and I thought it was the nicest lunch we'd ever had — then we saw Mr Rose as we came up Abbottsford Road, and he looked grave.

'May I speak to you, Ellinor?' he said, as he came opposite me. Mother took it that he was going to ask me to teach in Sunday school because of the need for teachers. She walked on ahead and he said to me, 'I have some bad news from the Front,' and I said, because I knew George was safe — he was in hospital in London, 'Not Harry?' and he said, 'Yes'.

'I can't speak to your mother,' he said. 'Will you tell her?'

I knew that I'd have to tell Mother. We went on slowly until we got to the house in Broughton Road, and Mother sank onto the couch and she said, 'My son, my son' — that's all she could say.

I was married in Sydney on Melbourne Cup Day, 1922. We had a house wedding. Our Strathfield house had a large double room — living room and dining room — so we opened back the folding doors and the dining table was put on the back verandah on the day of the wedding as there were such a lot of guests. My husband would have liked to go straight back to Flinders afterwards but I was determined we would have a honeymoon and we went to Leura in the Blue Mountains. Most of the men staying at Leura House changed into evening dress for dinner or at least their best suits. Bob made friends with one man and he said afterwards it was *such a relief to have a man to talk to*. But we did enjoy our honeymoon.

I rang Mother to tell her we were staying an extra week because Bob enjoyed it so much. When we'd been talking earlier about staying longer Bob said, 'I'll have to write home for some more money. I have to buy a pair of work boots,' and it was the first time I'd thought about what it would be like not to have ready money.

In 1922 our income was obtained from the sale of cheese and the Ayrshire stud cattle. We made cheese because there was no way for the fresh milk to be conveyed to Melbourne from Flinders as the nearest railway station was Bittern.

People didn't speak of the Depression. Those in the country had no more money than those in the city but they could grow their own vegetables. There had been a depression in the late 1880s but that was always referred to as 'the time the banks went broke', so the word depression perhaps wasn't used until 1930.

Connie Cragg, my cousin, used to say, 'You wealthy farmers out on Schanck Road,' . . . but she didn't know. Our friends the Meakins made their money out of potatoes. Anything for a living. Stan Meakin would leave at four in the morning to get to Victoria Market and catch the early buyers, for potatoes always grew well in the volcanic soil at Flinders.

We came to Wahring in 1931, my husband, myself, Andrew aged seven and Margaret aged five. All we had to bring with us was Queenie, a stock horse, and she wasn't young. When we first arrived we had to buy milk from Deane's across the paddocks until we were sent the best of the scrubbers from Flinders to fatten. So we moved from a good rainfall dairying area to mixed farming.

My mother would send money from Sydney, saying,

'Spend it on yourself,' and I would write and thank her very much for it and never say what it was spent on. I had to make £1 do a whole week and always we tried to be self-sufficient. We made a garden out of a paddock but water was a great problem.

The woman, as usual, carried the burden of the day. She had to be competent, to make her own clothes, to do all sorts of things. Lady Somers formed the Country Women's Association and the first Bush Nursing hospitals were opened in the late 1920s — a service taken for granted today.

The grocer trusted you and you could always get something to eat. The banks never trusted you too much. A great amount depended on the character of the man to whom they were lending money: but they too had to remember that even good men die young.

In our district, swagmen came through regularly. They would usually come in mid-morning, rolled grey blanket across the back, blackened billy and tin mug tied at the side. I would ask, 'Do you want the usual?' and that would be tea and milk and sugar. I buttered the bread because butter separately would have melted, and sometimes I had cold meat to give. Maybe the swaggie would split a barrowload of wood, maybe not. Perhaps they placed a stick or brick at the front gate in such a way that the next swagman knew his reception. They'd be along every six months or so but maybe they went north in the wintertime.

We had rabbits to eat and we killed our own lambs. Humidity in the summer was a problem because without refrigeration the animal had to be killed on a night which was reasonably cool. Every part of the sheep was used where possible and a leg might be put in brine. If you wanted to do more, a barrel had to be prepared by soaking so it wouldn't leak, but normally I prepared three gallons of brine in a kerosene tin. I put a plate weighted with a clean brick on top of the piece of meat until it became saturated with the brine, otherwise it would float.

My husband taught me to drive on the Flinders hills after dark; there was no time during the day. When the policeman from Mornington tested me, I had to drive from outside the bakery up to the monument and back. He said, 'I suppose I'll have to give you your licence,' and I said, 'I'll take you on the hills if you like.' I was confident driving there.

'No thanks,' he said, and then, 'I hope you won't be driving in the city for a while.'

My mother had given me a book called *The Family Doctor* and another book with illustrations (some of which she removed first) on my marriage. The children were brought up by the Truby King guidelines — of course there was no Infant Welfare Centre. How did we get to easy living?

But to do things with my hands always made me happy, especially when visitors were coming. Cooking, cleaning, polishing, gardening and bringing up children, were all very time-consuming in the 1920s.

Joan

Joan Larkin b.1900

IHAVE lived through the reigns of six monarchs — Victoria, Edward VII, George V, Edward VIII, George VI and Elizabeth II. This alone must surely make my nieces and nephews and my 'adopted families' think of me as an 'awfully old lady'.

Before I start to tell about my early life and memories I want to explain that I am trying to put into words all the things I want my dearly loved nieces and nephews (and others) to know: that I am not a rag doll with a sawdust inside and a wooden heart, and with sightless beads for eyes. I can see something of myself in every one of them; I have gone through the same broken messy romances, I have had my heart broken a few times and I have been cruel and broken hearts, too. I've loved madly, and I've hated madly. If they could only realise these things I am sure they would see they have much in common with their old aunt.

I have seen them all grow up, marry and have their kids. I have grown with their children also: every character so different — and a bit of me in all of them. Maybe I am sorry about that, though?

Right from childhood days I never really got on with my mum. I cannot honestly remember my mother ever talking to me, other than to make ordinary everyday remarks. I must say I respected her, and always thought she was beautiful especially when I was young. I seem to have such memories of her being beautifully dressed. Once when she was going to a wedding she wore a gorgeous white broderie anglaise frock and a large white leghorn hat with emerald-green fluffy feathers around it. Around her waist she wore a vivid emerald-green satin sash to match the feathers. Or the feathers to match the sash? She had a very good figure and carried herself well, even when she was old, and Father always told her when she looked nice. There were five girls in her family and they were all considered 'beauties' and I have heard this from other people who knew them when they lived in Cooktown (Queensland). Apparently they were very popular with the officers off the ships that my grandfather would pilot through Torres Strait. Until she died at seventy-nine years of age Mum was a fine-looking woman.

Dad adored Mum and not one of us would ever dare disobey or be rude to her (I know that I used to pull faces behind her back and my sister would tattletale and tell her what I had done). I don't ever remember her smacking me: she would leave that to Dad, and I know it was a proper threat — 'Wait until you father comes home!'

Yet Father was one of Nature's gentlemen. A gentle gentleman. He was nice to look at, nice to be with, never raised his voice in anger, but I always knew when I had done something that he did not approve of. He had the most beautiful clear blue eyes, and not one of us inherited this colour. We're all stuck with Mum's brown. He was always there when needed and loved us all, but Mother always came first. But behind that I knew he really put us almost on the same level — he was such a proud dad.

When I was four and my sister two we used to wait at the gate for Dad to come home from the office. We would climb up a smallish tree that bore both mandarins and oranges. I shall never forget the triumph when I would reach an orange and M. would get the mandarin! But because I climbed higher, she was always first down to greet Dad and get the first kiss and cuddle and be picked up and carried in up the front steps where Mother would be waiting. Then she, too,

Joan with younger sister

would kiss and cuddle that sister and that memory has never left me. M. and I have never got on — though as the years draw on we have become more tolerant: it is nice now because she often asks for my opinion on things, but before we never used to agree on anything. There was always the memory of Mother liking her better than me, and during my whole life that is how it seems to have been: Mother and M. together and me on the outside. Maybe this is childish to look back on, but it is there.

Mother once made me so damned furious I can still feel that fury, because at that particular time I had done my nursing training therefore I did know where babies came from, and I did have a good idea how it was done, too! M. who was married and living close by, and always seemed to be with Mother even if I only called in when passing, was nattering with Mother about a local lass who was expecting and I entered just as they were discussing childbirth, or whatever, and my mum said, 'Would you mind taking your cup of tea into the dining room, we are talking about something.'

And that generally was the way I was treated all along the line, until Dad died: and my heart broke for Mum. She was so lost and so alone, and I felt nothing but pity for her. I used to live rather a long way from her then but I would spend the day with her twice a week, and it would make me so terribly sad to say goodbye. She would stand at the gate and wave. I felt an awful heel and thought that I should stop with her until my brother came home, but time was short and I hated driving in the dark along a lonely bush road. I think that the eight to ten years when Mother lived without Dad was the only time that I had any feelings whatever about her — other than that she was Mum, and she always had my respect. Dad saw to that — he put her on a pedestal and, by golly, we had to do the same.

I don't remember her ever doing any housework. She always had a 'girl'. She never spoke of having a servant, it was always a 'girl', and there was one who even had grey hair. We children always had our meals in a breakfast room with the girl, Florrie or Minnie or Sigrid (who smelled a bit queer — ah! now I know what it was). But I remember Mother stirring the Christmas pudding, though I wouldn't mind betting a dollar that the girl had put it together for her. We all had a stir, and a good lick of the wooden spoon. But I think Mum was so cherished by dear old Father that the thought of her lifting a finger was out.

With help in the house, meals were always punctual and woe betide you if you weren't home to sit down when the bell rang. Even in my days of working in the city — which all fitted in with ferry times and whether Dad would be on a certain ferry — well bad luck, you had cold tea, or dinner, or whatever. Sunday nights we had to make our own meal and Mother and Father would take off to their own little part of the house, called 'Mum's Corner', a pretty sitting room at the end of the verandah. One of us would prepare their tea because, for as long as I can remember, we had midday dinner on Sundays, lovely roast meat and potatoes the like of which I've never tasted since.

Everything and everyone was so close in my childhood days. My paternal grandparents, two unmarried aunts and an uncle all lived near by and I spent a lot of time with Granny. I have always wanted to be like her, but we are all supposed to resemble Mother's family. Granny always wore black and a little lace cap on her hair, a chain round her neck with a locket on it: this held a snipping from each of her ten children's hair. I adored my aunt — thought she was beautiful then, but realised when I grew up that she was too plump and very frumpish as well. But she made a fuss of me, and loved me, and that was all I wanted in those days.

We lived in a house on stilts overlooking a bend in the Brisbane River. Our garden went right to the water's edge and we would all (three of us then) with Mum, troop down to the riverbank to wave to Uncle Henry, a purser on one of the passenger ships that plied between Brisbane, Townsville and Cairns — the AUSN line. The excitement was about who would spy Uncle Henry first. He always kept a large silk hanky (specially) to wave.

The cry from Mum, 'Here she comes, she's turning into the Reach,' (I never knew what a reach was of course, but once the ship turned everything was tense with excitement) and we jumped up and down madly as the ship went past and cried, 'There he is! There he is! I saw him first!' Then the fights would start — no, I did — and by the time the arguments had been settled the ship was well down the reach. My mother loved ships: she had been born at sea, in the Suez Canal. Her father was a sea captain and her mother used to sail with him. Most of Mother's sisters were born in foreign lands. Grandfather was also, at one time, a Torres Strait pilot, reputed to be able to take a boat through those waters with his eyes shut.

On Sundays we were always taken to church, in our best frocks — frilly, and always with a sash. It would not have been Sunday without a sash. St Mary's at Kangaroo Point is only slightly older than I am, which makes me feel even older than I am. It was such a long aisle to walk to our family pew at the front and be quiet when urged to giggle by cousins making faces at us as we passed their pews.

I went to St John's Cathedral Day School: co-educational, but all I remember about the boys was that they would chuck stones at us girls from the dividing fence in the play areas. I must have been a dill then because I was terrified I would be hit: later on in life I would have been straight into it, fists and all. Father worked in the church grounds, at the Diocesan Book Depot; we would travel in first by the small ferry across the river and then by tram up what used to be a big hill but now seems to have become a gentle slope. Often we just walked, and I always have thoughts of the green trees and the river: how often the lovely old Brisbane River is in my memories!

Once, in flood, it became terribly bogged down with water hyacinths. I can see it all now, the beautiful mauve water, the little tugs and the ships pushing their way through masses of flowers. One boat got stuck for ages, right in front of our place, and I can remember the propellers churning and churning, and being so upset because the flowers were getting thrown into the air. Granny and Grandfather used proudly to show us the watermark in their sitting room, 'It came right up to here,' and tell us stories of the Big Flood in the 1890s. When the house was repainted Granny insisted they leave the tide mark for posterity.

We had moved to Sydney when I went to work with Father, soon after I left school. We still lived by a river, the Lane Cove River, and travelled to and from town by ferry. In those days the ferries were like a club because everyone

Joan's picnic boat, Lane Cove

knew everybody else, and seats were left vacant — nobody
dared take certain seats until the ferry left the wharf and it
was understood that that passenger was not coming. I never
sat with Father; he insisted that I make friends with younger
folk — but when we got off at our wharf he would always
walk home with me, and always made sure to ask what sort
of day I'd had, even though I had been working with him, or
in the same office, all day. That was quite apart from being
Father — then, he was the Boss.

Father did a lot of good deeds that nobody ever heard
about; I know that when one of Mother's sisters was
widowed for the second time and left without much money,
Father saw that she had something each week for herself and
the children. He also helped her put another two through
school — but nobody ever heard tell of these matters. I
would know because of working with him, but he merely
said to me, 'We don't want everyone to hear about this, my
lass,' and that was that.

He was marvellous to me always. When I had a torrid love
affair (one of many), he was the only person I could turn to,
and though he couldn't really do much for me he did send
me to Brisbane to my brother for a year, and paid me a
weekly allowance — but with the proviso, 'Don't let your

mother know'. This was the general arrangement between Dad and me — keep it to yourself and nobody gets upset.

I loved him deeply and in this day and age I wonder if any of my nieces have the same affection for their father. Without him I would have been a very lonely girl at home. When Dad died something very very warm went from my life, and I have felt on the outside lines many times without his guiding hand to give a lift over the lousy patches.

I can remember the night Sydney Harbour was bombed — attacked by Japanese submarines. I was nursing privately at the time, and the baby was only three days old, and of course in those days the mother was never allowed out of bed for ten days or more, and treated as an invalid. Well, whenever you went to a case, you would always be briefed about where they intended to dash *if* we had an air raid. Luckily this night was well organised, and I had already got the pram set up with whatever we would need for the mother, baby and self. This husband was one of the ones I *have met* (*Husbands I Have Met* by J. Larkin), so I couldn't have cared less what happened to him (incidentally he was a doctor — one would have thought they would be above fun and games when the mum was busy producing, unfortunately in this case, a daughter, which didn't add to his pleasure at all).

Well, about the time that the babe would have to be bedded down, the sound of ghastly sirens wailed through the whole of Sydney. I can't express the sensation it gave, because of course we knew what to do, or thought we did, and had done all the classes we had to attend, but never in our wildest dreams I suppose, ever thought we would hear the real thing. My legs went to lolly water, the mother burst into tears, the babe was the only person actually calm for the few moments it took to get organised, and out the door I went with mother staggering on behind, me pushing the pram, with food and doings enough for a month, down into the odd sort of shelter at the end of a certain street.

The whole thing, although a nightmare for the short time it was on, became so hilarious. As we all mustered outside this shelter, you have never seen so many odd-looking people, some with blankets round them, some with hats on their heads although it was the middle of the night — I can remember one elderly chappie clutching his bottle of 'whusky', nothing would part him from that bottle. Anyway, to end the tale, before all the mob got into the shelter, the wardens doing their duty according to the book 'aged and children first', the siren went to give the All Clear.

The war lasted for so long, and there was so much that I did then — for one thing I eventually got myself a marvellous man, and married him. We were married in July and the war ended in the same year, but I remember that I had to cadge ration tickets, or cards, or whatever it was we had to have, to buy a new frock for the occasion, also shoes, I know that hats were on the free — and of all things, what did I deck myself out in — *blue*! And a lousy blue it was too, and why blue, because I have never even been a blue person — maybe at my age, forty-five, being a bride in blue was the accepted thing. It was a ghastly dress too, woollen, two-piece and very tailored, and I wore a stupid white felt hat — and I hate hats.

It took such a long time for me to get this special husband, though nobody could say I didn't have a good time looking for him because I had a ball — and some of the things I did my beloved nieces might be doing now, well, great nieces actually, and of course I would throw up my hands in horror, and be terrified.

Sandy

Sandy Douglas b.1906

WHEN I was seven years old I was given a First Aid book to look at: an acute attack of tonsillitis was keeping me in bed. During my mother's absence a friend who was studying First Aid was looking after me.

'Has she been good?' asked my mother.

'Well, I haven't done much study, she hasn't let go of that book.'

From then on, my dolls always had some part of their bodies in bandages or splints.

My father had come to Coolgardie from Victoria in the late 1880s to try his luck on the new goldfields. My mother and older brother Jack followed him later when he had established a home. Mother and Father had been Salvation Army officers in the days when that organisation had very little money. As a young captain, twenty-one years old, Mother remembered tying the soles of her shoes on with string. She had met my father at the Exhibition Building in Melbourne when they both sang in a quartet. Dad had a good tenor voice and Mother a good contralto.

After the deaths of her first two children Mother suffered a nervous breakdown and they no longer carried on as leaders, but Mother's interest in the Army remained till her death. Her name was Eva Messenger.

I was born in Fremantle but we later moved to a house at

the junction of the Norseman and Kalgoorlie Roads. It was a timbered-frame with iron roof, hessian walls — some painted and others papered. Texts hung on some of the walls, and a picture of an angel with outstretched wings as if protecting two small children who were crossing over an old bridge. We were brought up to believe somebody up above was also watching over us besides our parents.

If my parents had arguments it was never in front of me. My belief was that parents slept together so they could speak privately.

Everything in our house shone. 'Elbow grease and turpentine, that's the thing to make it shine,' I heard more than once. The black stove was Mother's pride. It could not have been brighter. The big water boiler with its long stem and brass tap on the end, the heavy iron saucepans, the fender with its brass surrounds, all gleamed.

The mantelpiece was too high for me to reach unless I stood on a chair, but after all that trouble there was nothing much of interest there; the clock with its chimes, a half stick of Bates Salve, a money box (mustn't be touched), receipts, accounts to be paid, and a bottle of Dr Morse's Indian Root Pills — the only medication I ever knew my father to take. He chewed charcoal for his teeth and at eighty still had quite a few, though I doubt had a dentist seen them he'd have encouraged Father to keep them.

I wasn't always a happy child. My only mates lived across a paddock of high dry grass and prickles. I wasn't encouraged to join the boys in their outings. In fact they wouldn't let me go with them.

I used to feel I had been born into the wrong family and sometimes would wonder if they owned me or should I really belong to a family with lots of money. I was tired of being poor, wearing other girls' passed-on dresses. Once a child's hat blew out of the train window. But why did I have to have it? I hated the woman who gave it to Mother. I hated the hat. And more than all, I hated that unknown kid who so carelessly let it blow out. I didn't wear it many times; I lost it too.

I would make up stories when I went to bed of what would

Sandy with mother and Roy

happen when I grew up. I wouldn't do any work. I would have lots of children and live in a two-storeyed house; I would eat only what I liked, and buy my own clothes.

Our home didn't have a bathroom: the back room with floor scrubbed white served as one with a dish on the tankstand for hand washing. Bath night in winter, the copper was lit, the water carried through the porch door and two more doors, then tipped into a galvanised tub in front of the fire. There was always an argument between my brother and I as to who would go first and I wasn't allowed to look.

The memory of seeing my first real bathroom has always remained. A room built just to bath and wash in! A bath so big an adult could lie full length in it! There was no carrying of water; taps marked hot and cold and the hot water was right there; and nobody had to get in after you. It was fascinating to watch the water swirl round and disappear when the plug was pulled out. It did seem a waste not to put it on the flowers. I thought my aunt must be very rich. Then, to be dried with a lovely soft white towel. It must be the nearest approach to heaven.

At one time my father owned what was termed a 'puddler'. There were lots of offers of gold obtained in various ways — all he would have to do was put it through the puddler and who would be any the wiser? But he kept on trying the hard way, the honest way.

Everything in my childhood depended on the crushing.

'Yes, we will try and get it for you when the crushing goes through.'

Quite often when expenses were met, there was nothing left for extras and we were back where we started.

There was a time we owed some money at the grocer's: most people did. We also needed some stores.

'Go up the street and ask the grocer if we could have a small order; I know we owe something but we will fix the account as soon as we can and don't forget to say "please".'

I didn't know the word was humiliation; I know I felt terribly ashamed. The grocer did give me the stores: he knew we would pay *when things looked up*.

Mother was a careful housekeeper. She had to be. We never opened a tin — they were for prospectors going out into the bush.

'Sausages? Never. You don't know what is in them.'

There were some large pipes over the other side of the line.

'I think Nigger has a rabbit bailed up, Mum,' Roy would say.

'Well, you had better go and see.'

In that manner he escaped his nightly chores, but catch them he did. We had braised rabbit, baked, stewed and curried rabbit: every method in and out of the recipe book. It was no good for us to get tired of our fare. Until something turned up we preferred it to goat. Our own chooks I wouldn't eat. Everything alive was a pet.

In all my years spent in the outback I have only sighted one snake, and that was moving fast out of my way. Years later I nursed Rocky Vane the snake collector and was fascinated with his snakeskin waistcoat. But a dead snake is the best sort of snake I think.

When Jack worked on a farm he once sent us a piglet. Roy and I loved that pig. We couldn't get home from school fast enough to let it out of its sty. When Mother was absent we would let it run through the house. When the butcher finally came for it, no promises could compensate for its loss. Years later, after many tests, I was found to be allergic to pork. The mind is a delicate piece of mechanism . . .

The table set for Sunday night's tea was a picture; the beautifully laundered tablecloth with swans embossed in the linen, the blue cut-glass sugar basin on a leg and with a jam dish to match, the bread board — scrubbed so often that the word 'bread' was scarcely visible. In the middle sat the white kerosene lamp with its glass chimney holding a bent hairpin — stopped it from smoking we were told. There was a high sponge cake with lemon filling: no cream, we didn't even get cow's milk. Always there were scones, butter and jam, cold meat, cut up salad with home-made mayonnaise and there was beetroot. I was always afraid of dropping that on the tablecloth, so passed that by.

No unnecessary work was done on Sundays. Time was spent only on going to Sunday school and church. The roast, if we had one, was always cooked on Saturday: cold on Sunday and anything left made into stew on Tuesday. We always had sufficient to eat.

One day Roy said to me, 'You go up over the hill to school. I am going up the town way.'

At recess time word got about that he had found two shillings. It sounded a small fortune to me. He sought me out and gave me some of the chocolate he'd bought. They were Toblers and in each chocolate was a card. He was trying to get a full set, and that was why he'd bought all chocolate.

I couldn't get home quickly enough to tell Mother of Roy's good fortune: she wasn't nearly as excited as I. She looked sad and didn't answer. She knew where the two shillings intended for the paper man had gone.

Roy got a belting; I was called a pimp, but the thought of him stealing had never occurred to me. He told Mother, I remember quite plainly, 'Other boys have money to spend.' He did save us a lot by catching rabbits, so from then on he got some money to spend each week.

My lesson in honesty was somewhat different, nevertheless never forgotten. A girl of my own age and I were walking home from school when she stumbled and fell. A man driving a draught horse pulling a dray got down, picked her up and gave her sixpence. I would hate to think I took it from her forcibly, but the sixpence arrived home with me. My mother questioned me: she had an uncanny knack of knowing the truth. She made me sit down and write a letter to the mother. I can remember the very part of the table I sat at and with the aid of the kerosene lamp confessed my guilt.

What an effort that was: I was fully convinced the loan of the sixpence wasn't worth the effort it caused. I must have practically thrown both letter and sixpence to the mother as I never had any recollection of her face. The lesson lasted me a lifetime.

Sometimes I was left home with Dad at night: I loved that. He would make toffee or pancakes, sometimes chipped potatoes. He had lovely curly hair and one night he let me cut some of his curls off to stick on my baldheaded doll. Mother was not amused and sent him smartly to the barber's next day to get tidied up.

The dentist from Kalgoorlie came down periodically to attend patients in our town. He must have been one of the few people around who owned a motor car. On this occasion he ran into our fence, knocked part of it down but made no attempt to compensate us. My brother had to take me to have a tooth extracted.

'When the dentist asks you for money tell him he knocked over our fence and you haven't any money.' This I did.

'Well, well. I will have to see about that,' and he ruffled my hair.

Roy offered him the shilling: the price of an extraction in those days. I didn't know it had been given to him. The dentist refused it and did call to see Dad about the fence.

We lived on the edge of an area called Fly Flat. There were still plenty of flies but not a square inch of land one could call flat. It had been turned over so many times in search of that elusive gold. There were quite a number of elderly men living on the area: little camps made out of beaten-out kerosene tins clamped together, all rusty but for all our violent storms I never knew one to blow down. They were only large enough for their bunk, table, box to sit on and a meat safe. I never went in one but could just see into them through the smoke haze of their fires. The men were contented and independent searching for their gold, however small the amount.

One man told me he would take me around the world when his ship came in. The largest stretch of water I had seen was the dam. He also had a puddle of water near his camp and I thought this was where it would come in. I would skip down every few days.

'Has your ship come in yet?'

'No, but it will one day, lass, and we will be on it.'

Most of them had Irish names. There was Tommy Tanguey, known as the 'mayor of the Three Mile': he was a real con-man. Would take a chook up to the pub, sell it, stay and drink the proceeds, go around the back and take possession of the bird once again, perhaps to sell it at another hotel or return home. They knew he did it, but his victims felt his humour was worth letting him think he was taking them for a ride.

Once he was on a charge at court. His goats had eaten the flowers in the Presbyterian Manse.

'Do you plead guilty, or not guilty?'

'Not guilty, your honour, those goats are good Irish goats and would only eat what's green.'

There was Bill McFadden whose shirt shone with grease. It was said, on being admitted to hospital, another shirt was found underneath and the hairs of his chest had grown through it. I didn't know whether it was true or not, but that's what the adults said.

Mrs Hennessy went past the back of our house every day. On her way back she was always a bit tottery. I thought she must have been very tired. Roy and I played a stupid trick on her. Along the path she walked we dug a small hole, covered it with paper and then sand. We hid behind a mine dump to watch: but she didn't fall down, only one leg went through the paper. We giggled; she used language I had never heard before and went over to the house to complain about 'those varmints o' yourn'.

But I must have been impressed. The road near our house had become very boggy after some rain. A teamster was whipping some big horses: they were doing their best. I went out and shouted, 'If you don't stop belting those horses I'll bloody well tell my father on you, you bugger.' I didn't repeat this to my family but the driver later said to my father, 'You have a bit of a spitfire in that girl of yours.'

Dad could scarcely believe it, but not letting me down he answered, 'Yes, I think she has inherited something from my Irish mother.'

The school I attended was a pretty building made of local pink stone. I attended a 'Back to Coolgardie' in 1969. It was the seventy-fifth anniversary of the school. I sat in my very same seat. Although at its peak more than 520 pupils attended there the number in 1969 had dropped to fifty. It was so strange to hear, 'Oh hello, you sat next to me fifty years ago in this classroom.'

I had a good walk around the town: everything looked diminished in size, excepting wide Bayley Street. I looked at the bridge under which no train goes now, the line being diverted via Bonnie Vale. It was on this bridge I received my first kiss at seventeen. He and his friend had accompanied my girlfriend and me home from the pictures: unasked by me, it was my friend they knew.

'My mother wouldn't like that,' said I.

'I'm not kissing your mother, I'm kissing you.'

It stirred nothing in me. I still had to wait some time for that. Without meaning, like that it was cheap I thought.

During my schooldays I was not the most brilliant in class. In fact one teacher told me, 'I do not know what you think you are going to do with your life.'

They had a great love of caning in those days or hitting you on the hands with a thick ruler. I had no head for mental sums and after each question, if your answer was wrong, you had to stand up, hold out your hand and get the 'cuts'. I was a nervous child. My mother said to me, 'Next time it happens tell the teacher to try it on her own self.'

Everything my mother said was right so I repeated this to the teacher, who immediately retorted, 'Stay in at recess time.'

'Why were you cheeky to me?'

'I didn't mean to be cheeky but it makes me sick when I get the cane.'

It was at another school, in Highgate Hill, that I received a prize for the most improved pupil of the year. It was a thrill to hear my name called out. But I loved the teacher I had then, and felt she liked me.

The second year of the 1914-18 war, a young monitor teacher asked the class, 'Hand up anybody who can't bring a shilling for the Red Cross.'

My brother Roy, a class higher but in the same room, promptly put up his and nodded to me to do likewise.

'Why can't you bring a shilling, Sanfead?'

'Because my brother is at the war and my father is going too, my mother needs all her shillings.'

I was so proud of my brother and of my father when he, too, went into khaki. I remember holding his hand on the way to our Sunday school anniversary. There had been a violent storm and hailstones as big as bantam's eggs piled up along the fence. Some of us collected them in our handkerchiefs and took them with us up onto the dais. When they dripped down onto the ones in front we couldn't have been very popular.

My life was good. I was loved, although at times I didn't think so. I remember a time we had an epidemic of diphtheria and a little boy died. We were given a half day off to go to his funeral: we were all very sad and mystified. That night I held the blankets tightly over my head and held my breath. The only reason I can think of is I wished to cause attention and craved to be *somebody* even if dead. Once I remember my mother saying to my father, 'Why have you got your best pants on? If you had to go to a funeral you would have nothing to wear.'

The troop trains went by our house. Khaki-clad figures would be hanging out of all the windows, some would throw me kisses, comic cuts and little posies they had been given at Kalgoorlie. I thought they all looked as happy as the children on the Fresh Air League trains going for a holiday to the sea. I didn't really understand what it was all about nor why they were going to kill the Germans. In the Bible my mother had read to us, 'Thou shalt not kill'.

The night before Jack sailed on the *Mindoola* on 23 November 1915, there was a party at his girlfriend's house. All the most morbid songs were sung. My poor mother, with her eldest son going off to war, had to sit and listen to young people bellowing out exuberantly, 'Just before the battle, Mother, I was thinking most of you'. How her heart must have been breaking. He was so handsome with beautiful eyes and a good strong face full of character. He was eighteen years old.

We knew when he was wounded. I came out into the kitchen and said, 'I dreamt about Jack. He had a bandage around his head and his arm in a sling.' Mother received a telegram from the War Office which verified it. She said, 'At least God has spared him. We must be happy for that.' We went to meet him at Fremantle but the wounded men were taken in cars to the Base hospital. We picked him out as they travelled slowly by.

'Oh dear,' said Mother, 'he has learned to smoke.' She had to say something to distract us from the sight of the shield over the socket of the eye no longer there.

I can remember the ladies in their best clothes, long white skirts and blouses, hats. In the train going to Fremantle nobody spoke: it was as serious as church. Then there was the bunting and the cheering, but to everybody there was only one face they were looking for.

Writing this I have realised more the dreadful unbearable heartbreaks those mothers must have gone through. Those words come back to me:

> 'If I was hanged on the highest tree,
> Who would be there?
> My mother.'

Father and Jack came home within a day of each other. We received official word of Jack's return, but the advice of Father's arrived later than he did. How disappointed he must have been, nobody to meet him. My mother was at a funeral and found Father home when she returned.

I was shy with them: they had been away out of our lives and I felt they seemed so serious and knew so much.

Father put his age down from fifty-four to forty-five when he enlisted because of Jack's disastrous wound. But Jack was furious and Father's commanding officer just happened to be a personal friend of his.

'You have a man in your Unit old enough to be my father.'

'How can you prove it?'

'He is my father.'

Dad was offered a position with the Red Cross Supply Branch. Nothing doing. If he couldn't be right in amongst the fighting he preferred to return to Australia. It took him a long time to forgive his son.

Jack is eighty-six now, a very alert man, and wears a dark lens over the eye socket: it was too smashed to accept a glass eye without a lot of embarrassment.

Father had one or two good jobs after long spaces without work. Finally his feet got itchy for the goldfields again. Gratuity Bonds were hard to cash: they had to be taken out in kind. So it was a new suit for him, and also for Roy who went into his first long pants. My gift was a leather suitcase with gold initials on it for school. The Gratuity Bond was worth £80.

His first job had been working on the switchback road to City Beach. His hands were soft. They blistered and bled and then formed calluses. Then he was employed at the Post Office store on night duty. But the call back to his old haunts was like a needle to a magnet. He discussed it many times with Mother.

'One just needs the break and you have a fortune.'

'We have been through all that before.'

She firmly believed we would never get rich quick. How right she was, but as Father said, 'It's worth a try'.

The Spanish Flu was at its height. Blackboy Camp was reopened to take the sick. People staying at home had a person watching outside that nobody entered or left the building. It was a notifiable disease. Our nextdoor neighbour died. His wife came in to Mother, who put her apron over her mouth and went in and did the necessary things. She never spoke about that to me. She simply said on her return, 'Don't come near me until I have had a hot bath, washed my clothes and put on fresh ones.'

There could not have been any guard there, they apparently had not reported.

Children wore camphor bags round their necks. You caught it or you didn't, but if unfortunate enough to catch it the patient often died. So the city was a place one was happy to get out of.

Father returned to Coolgardie, was offered and he accepted and held the mail contract from Coolgardie to Ora Banda for some years: first with four horses and an open buggy, later a converted Ford car. Once he broke his arm and was put into Kalgoorlie hospital.

'Did I swear while coming out of the anaesthetic?'

'No. You only said "Get up Brownie you renegging old cow".' Brownie had been his horse least inclined in carrying the King's mail. Why he asked that I don't know: he didn't drink and he didn't smoke and I never heard him swear. But maybe he felt like it often and did do a swear when he was on his own.

Mother felt it was no life for men on their own. Roy had joined Father already and so, at the age of fifteen, I returned to the old camp. Life was monotonous for the young: I went to Kalgoorlie once a week for music lessons, sometimes in Lizzie but often on the express — it was only 25 miles and the express was more reliable.

73

Lizzie had a habit in a deep sand patch of turning right round. One day we went when the Coolgardie races were on. The road was a dirt road and narrow. Every time Father heard a car coming towards him he would pull over into the bush and wait until the oncoming car had passed. Our progress was slow.

Part of the four years Mother spent back in Coolgardie I stayed with Jack and his wife at Fremantle. Jack was a foreman on the Peel Estate to a group of migrants. They only grew potatoes — the scheme was a failure. Such desolate country. If only those migrants who returned to England could see the luscious gardens and beautiful homes that are there now, they would be surprised. Some of the men didn't even know how to harness a horse. The soil, only sand, needed a lot of building up with superphosphate and blood and bone manure. The best land was swamp land and apparently the Government didn't have the money to drain it.

Although I enjoyed the break away from the goldfields with younger people, so often I have begrudged the time I spent away from Mother. We were like close friends, almost sisters, though she never talked about the private life between a man and a woman. Many girls these days know more at thirteen and younger, than I did at twenty. There was a house in the town that men used to visit and, though I never understood why, on my way home from school I used to pass it hurriedly with a feeling of awe and bewilderment.

From Perth to Fremantle on the train there were a number of little latticed houses that we passed. If men occupied the carriage I never looked, nor any of the other females. But if there were 'ladies only', furtive glances would be made during the few seconds it took to pass them.

I was once sent down to a friend's place: she would tell me something I should know. My friends, Eva and Hazel, had found a Home Nursing Book in their mother's wardrobe, with coloured pictures of babies being born. We spent our time looking at these. I went home no wiser on the subject I was expected to learn. The coloured pictures remained in my mind a jumbled mess for a couple of days, then were forgotten. My mother never asked me if I was any wiser.

Then, for no given reason, Mother and I returned to Perth leaving the men behind. In a very short time she became ill and died six weeks after an operation. I was twenty years old.

Now I was on my own. I had two choices: to return to Melbourne with my aunt who would provide a home for me, or stay and steer my own course. I chose the latter.

Having been taught housework thoroughly in view of one day having a home of my own, domestic work was thrust upon me. The position was as good as I could have found anywhere.

I was told I did not sweep floors as well as my predecessor. That worried me not at all. Had I known, by the time I had completed my Junior Nursing time, the miles of floors I had swept would have put me in the running for a gold medal. Then the housekeeper who looked after the elderly lady became ill and a trained nurse was employed meanwhile.

'Why are you here doing domestic work?' she asked me.

'Because I haven't a home.'

'Would you like to do nursing?'

'Oh yes, but then one needs a good education.'

'Not necessarily. Do a correspondence course and obtain your entrance certificate.'

'Oh I will!' I told her with much enthusiasm.

In a few months I had begun a career to which I became dedicated for forty-two years.

Alice

Alice McKenzie b.1900

MY grandparents came to Australia in the 1850s. In 1856, while the gold rush was still on, James Barling opened a store at Bulla. But that didn't suit him. Six o'clock rising to open wasn't for him. Sir Rupert Clarke, who was a great friend, persuaded him to teach. He was appointed to Marong where he and his wife Louisa raised a family of nine. When my father, Walter, finished school he was given a choice — apprenticeship to a dentist or a bootmaker. He chose to be a bootmaker.

After marrying Sarah Ingham whose family came from Guildford, my father opened a bootmaker's shop in Smith Street, Fitzroy. In those days Smith Street was the busiest, most thriving street in Melbourne, with Foy's store on both sides of the street. Twice a year, Foy's Fair was the biggest attraction in town: tram loads of people just poured in and the Foy delivery vans were busy for weeks afterwards. Those same lorries were our transport every Melbourne Cup day. Two church seats were placed back to back in the middle of an open lorry, with vans for carrying the smallest children so they wouldn't fall out.

We set off in a great convoy, along Smith Street, then to the country (we all thought). We actually went to Studley Park, only a short distance from Melbourne. Our annual Sunday school picnic was the highlight of our year, such a lovely place, a river and trees and grass to run on, races and all.

I was the second of five girls, all born in Smith Street. We lived at the back of and over the shop. At 8 p.m. my father put up the shutters over the glass front, fastening them with two iron bars.

My whole family were involved in all the church activities. My earliest memories are of rows of my mates and me, with about three teachers. We sang hymns and listened to Bible stories, waiting to be released. The row of littlies who sat with the straightest backs, arms folded in front, was always sent out first.

From the age of three I longed to go to school. My oldest sister was always 'top of the class'. I thought that meant she could walk over all the rest. I was sent when I was four. We had slates, pencils and primers. Slates had to be cleaned with a damp rag. Teacher's command 'Clean slates', was followed by a quick whip round to see if anyone spat on his slate.

Our teacher was young, with long hair tied at the back with a very large black ribbon. Every dress she wore was patched, especially on the elbows with new material which showed up, but she was very pretty we thought.

How very quiet were my childhood days with horse-drawn carts and carriages, and four-wheeled cabs and hansom cabs. To ride in one of those one had to be rich. The driver perched very high at the back, reins in hand going over the roof to the horse. The cab held only two people who had a sort of waterproof apron to pull up. Roads were either dusty or muddy. Skirts had to be grasped at the back of the knees and swung round above shoe height. No lady would swing it above her ankles.

Our entertainment was all connected with the church, where we went to all services on Sundays, with various concerts in the Sunday school hall. A great innovation during our teens was the introduction of dances in the hall, which led to the 'wowsers' in the congregation becoming very vocal about wickedness. They couldn't have seen some of our romping games we played at socials.

Once a week we Sunday school girls would go to a meeting of people calling themselves the 'Sew-ers Band'. There we threaded beads for the heathen. Whoever was there first had the pick of the boxes which meant she had the largest beads so was finished first. My sisters and I were all taught piano. I had a good ear and a long memory which kept me busy at the piano all my life.

Early this century Melbourne was well provided with public transport — the cable trams. These were in two parts, the front or 'dummy' being the operational bit, the power being an ever-running cable under the road. To start, the brake was released, a hook dropped down to grip the cable, the driver pulled a rope overhead to ring a clanger and both vehicles moved off. The pace allowed intending passengers to run alongside and swing up on to either the platform of the car or the dummy where the passengers sat with backs to the driver in the middle. The driver was called the grip-man. I wonder if the grip-man was paid extra for being exposed to the weather or if the conductor received danger money because, as the tram went round a corner, it was his duty to stand on the open-ended platform, arms spread out to prevent passengers falling out.

'Mind the curve,' he'd call out.

My teenage years were very busy: walking to a big school where I was teaching — George Street, enrolment 750, going to night school at Melbourne High to catch up on training which I had missed, choirs, church activities, tennis, theatres. During the winter when we couldn't play tennis we'd walk to the city to a matinee. We had to be early, then when the doors opened we'd run up the stairs to the 'gods'. Many a good play or musical we saw for the price of sixpence or a shilling.

After four years of pupil teaching, because I hadn't trained any further I had to apply for a small country school, or stay on a salary of £65 a year. A group of us went to the Teachers' Training College for a fortnight where a marvellous old teacher showed us how to manage a group of thirty pupils of all ages and grades.

At the end of the two weeks each prospective head

teacher of a one-teacher school had to take over for a lesson. I chose singing. Mr Brown said, 'You're the first I've ever had to do that for me.' When I had the children all singing a round of 'Row, row, row your boat, gently down the stream', he was delighted. Singing wasn't his forte so 'God Save the King' was their only tune, sung on Monday mornings when the whole school 'saluted the flag':

'I love God and my country,
I honour the flag,
And will cheerfully obey my parents,
    teachers, and the law'

with right hand over the heart.

After letters had been exchanged with the committee of the Cobaw school, enrolment eleven, I set out by train for Woodend, (72 km from Melbourne) in November 1920. There I was met by a little old man who said he was the mailman, who was to drop me at Cobaw, 18 kilometres away. His vehicle was a very old jinker, a two-wheeled job, with iron tyres. It looked as though it was held together by string, but it must have been wire. I had never been to the country and was determined not to show my ignorance so put my foot on the high step and scrambled aboard. My suitcase was put where I would have expected my feet to be, so I sat with them on top of the case. Then we drove to the post office where we waited for the mail bags, then to a shop where we picked up bundles of newspapers, some of which were placed on my end of the seat, so I perched on top. After adding various parcels, and wrapped bread, we set off. A few miles out we were met by an old lady driving an even more decrepit vehicle with an even older horse, but she took some of the bundles of papers and parcels, to deliver them in another direction.

I was met at Cobaw by my prospective landlady who proved to be a remarkable woman, who used her spare time doing exquisite needlework. I think the amount of farm work she could cover coloured my ideas of what farmers' wives were expected to do forever.

I walked the mile to school next morning where I was met by the eleven pupils, a very shy but sturdy lot. The stone school and one house were the only buildings. I wondered whatever I'd do at weekends — no books anywhere, nothing to do, no place to go. But a friend of a friend arrived on the Friday, driving a horse and jinker with rubber tyres and padded seats and I soon met others from the little village.

Sometimes the parents held a dance in the school, to music provided by a dear old man with a fiddle. He was good, too, but not always available. So I asked the committee of five men if we could buy a piano. They really were a lovely lot though I never could understand why they were farmers. Wherever they met, and whoever was there, they complained about the weather, the crops, the sheep, the prices, and the weather, always.

We each put in £5 for a piano and got one for £45. Then I had to play for all the dances in our little one-roomed country school. The young people always came from the towns around.

When the 1914 war started (whoever would have thought then that it would become known as the First World War) everyone was bewildered. We used to visit my favourite cousin in camp at Broadmeadows, rows of tents with plenty of horses about. We soon learnt the meaning of 1st Light

Horse, Brigades, and then — Gallipoli. We weren't to know the horror for some time. Then, when the casualty lists began to come out, hundreds waited outside the *Herald* and *Argus* offices until lists were posted up, a nervewracking experience. It was days before we knew just where our soldiers were, some of them having had only a few weeks of training.

Soon after we were at war, a wave of hatred swept the country. Germans were hunted, shop windows smashed, but we never heard of internments. A nice old German couple living near us went into hiding in their house, coming and going through their back gate for their shopping. Then one day they just disappeared, leaving all their belongings. They may have been interned. Some Germans sold their homes very cheaply, a deposit of £100 and a promise to pay them the rest, and it was yours. A jeweller near us made a small fortune this way.

We heard ghastly stories about the cold and mud in the trenches, the wonder was that any of these soldiers lived to get home. My cousin went all through the war, but he would never talk about it.

I was only eighteen when it ended. Great crowds celebrated in the streets, cheering, waving flags and singing 'Rule Britannia'. We walked to the city, heard that the Town Hall was open to anyone, and there was to be a free concert. Dame Nellie Melba walked up to the platform and sang 'Home Sweet Home' and 'God Save the King'. Then the crowd sang it with her.

Margaret

Margaret Oliver b.1898

THE time: early 1918. The place: Newcastle, England. All my nearest and dearest prayed for me in church and Ma's parting words were, 'Don't get near the firing line and don't go out with men.'

Pa reassured her, 'She'll battle through; she's too daft to do anything else.'

The pockets of my uniform were nearly on my knees but when I complained to the officer in charge that I would be better without pockets, she said, 'No, dear. You will see that you can get nearly round the world with what you put in them.' And she was right.

My time in the WAAC (Women's Army Auxiliary Corps) in France would fill a book. (It has. Ed.) During that time our life was lived at two levels — one was our day-to-day working and playing, and at the other, a terrible anxiety for our lads. The Big Push had started. One heard of wins at Mons, and Ypres and Arras, and the trains of wounded (on the way to Le Havre) had only the front for them now, the rear wagons were full of enemy prisoners. Some of them were so young, we wondered what their parents were feeling. But at least these boys would get home. And *please God*, let *our* lads survive the coming months.

On some of the lovely summer days we used to discover the surroundings of Le Havre, which were varied and beautiful. Then, like a miracle, leave lists were posted and our lot were to leave at the beginning of November and, oh, the excitement. We ironed our hat brims, pressed coat-frocks and top coats, bought new stockings, packed our haversacks and suitcases, and waited, hardly daring to breathe. But at last we were at the station, doing what we usually did, waiting and waiting for the train to go. The weather was cold and we perished on the platform until a friend let us have a drop of Malaga which she had intended to take home.

We stopped at Amiens and were allowed a short time to walk around but, after seeing the Cathedral all sand-bagged up and the famous rose window boarded up to keep out the weather as the window itself had been safely buried, I didn't want to see further. We had seen many of the shattered houses and it was awful — rooms sliced off, some of the pictures still on the walls, and dresses and other oddments hanging over the edges of the ruins. When we got back to the train I kept wondering if the folks were killed in the barrage or had they escaped. A Tommy told me, 'They were evacuated a while before the Jerries got through, and I'm afraid we did a lot of damage blowing them out of it but no civilians were hurt, except where some would not leave . . . they may have been caught.'

My misery stayed with me until we got to Boulogne, and then we saw a huge roaring stove in the middle of a big hall. I was the first one to get to it. We had a meal and then we again saw the sea, and our packet boat alongside the wharf.

All the family were at the station to meet me and what a reunion! But only one among the many; for most of the boys it was their first leave in a long time. Stirring days lay ahead for me, visiting and being visited, trips to the cinema (films were black and white and silent), and every shop having a news board in the window telling us how the war was moving. And move it did.

On the morning of 11 November I had been doing some household shopping when a loud hailer shouted the news of 'Armistice!' and outside all the offices and shops crowds

Improperly dressed: 2s 6d fine for low neck, jewellery and hairstyle

gathered to listen to the news being passed on by hailer from the telephone. We had no radio in those days but it was amazing how quickly the news got round. I had a job getting home and jumped into the small hallway yelling, 'It's signed, Armistice! It's signed!' Then the doormat shot from under me and I fell flat on my back at the foot of the stairs. Mother dashed along the passage and said, 'I should have told you. I polished the floor.'

Everybody said of course now I would not have to go back to France, but suddenly I wanted to be back among my friends and communal life, and I was glad to go back. There would be clearing up to be done and work was not just going to come to a full stop.

Our staff was put on to working out the peacetime needs for the future, making lists of consumed equipment for the worst three years of the war. We were now allowed to stay out until 9 p.m. (roll call had been at 8.30 p.m.) and later on, the ban on dances was lifted. Before Armistice there had been a directive 'No dances will be allowed for the Forces as these are likely to inflame the passions of the troops' and an

Meg (seated) with friend

added note 'A free supply of lime juice will be issued to all personnel'! When I asked Ginger, my offsider, how his passions were coping and had he had his lime juice today, he said bitterly, 'Don't get enough grub to gimme strength for that kind of hanky panky.'

At our first 'do' on Christmas Eve we were allowed to wear our overalls with a coloured bow at the neck, and could keep going till 10.30 p.m. No lack of partners there and a good time was had by all. Refreshments were cheese sandwiches and mugs of lemonade, but dancing was the thing: the dining hall of Hostel No. 4 had a paved floor. Our social life took off with a real rush.

The various military camps, now demobilisation centres, were allowed to have dances and could invite twenty or thirty of us — usually taken in a lorry accompanied by an older F/W* — but everybody had to be out promptly by

---

* F/W — Forewoman. We lower order were 'workers' in the Women's Army Auxiliary Corps and after a row about our duties in the army, where someone had written home and said we were called 'soldiers' comforts', and we were there for one reason only, we were made 'Queen Mary's Army Auxiliary Corps'.

9.30 p.m. The Aussie dances were very popular; they had a lovely drill hall kept polished for dancing by a group of German prisoners. Anyone who loved dancing as I did was always on the list.

One night in a figure dance I was looking over my partner's shoulder when a laddie in the next couple stared at me as if he was startled, and then said, 'How did *you* get here?' My turn to be surprised but my answer, 'The same as anyone else' seemed to settle him down . . . perhaps my slightly Geordie accent did the trick, and we finished the dance.

He came straight over. 'You are so like my sister that I thought . . . well, it gave me a shock.'

I suppose I must have grinned for he said, 'Well, if I could meet you I could bring her photos.' I thought this was fair so we met the following Sunday and, truly, Maidie was my double. My room mates howled with laughter at me, and said it was a new way of getting a date with a WAAC. But I liked Guy and we were very much in harmony from the first. He played the violin in their dance band and I played the piano whenever I got the chance, and we both had the same kind of caring backgrounds. That was how we became good friends, and it was quite a while before we felt there must be something more later.

So we went to dances, and hiked all over the countryside, went to the 'Crystal Palace' (the YMCA) for teas — usually a mug of tea, bread and margarine and a boiled egg, but a change from barrack meals. Sometimes there were shows at the CP and then came a mad dash round the block to get in for roll call, now greatly daring at 9 p.m.

We girls used to watch from our small balcony to see the last tram going past the end of our Place Gambetta and it was as good as a circus. The trams were small but had one or two trailers, and as it was the only transport for the Aussie camp, the last one was a picture — covered with Aussies, tram and trailers full inside and dozens of the lads hanging on the outside and also sitting on the couplings and finally on the roofs. When a Digger was spotted running for the tram, the roof dwellers merely pulled the trolley off the line and amid loud streams of French from down under the latecomers were hauled on board. It was a nightly performance and the MPs turned a blind eye, and after a resounding cheer for our benefit, the whole rowdy lot disappeared in the direction of Harfleur and Montevilliers.

We were all very young and noisy and happy in those immediate post-war days — irresponsible I suppose, but enjoying just being alive. And now we were being invited to all the Army units in Havre, including a rather small camp where the Argyle and Sutherland Highlanders were being kept before demobilisation. We did a lot of Scottish dances and as there were about fifty players in their band they took up nearly half of the YMCA hut, but we did very well with the other half for dancing. And at intervals the pipers would take over to give them a rest. I don't know what the locals living near thought of the din. I can still hear the hooches as we spun around and the thud of boots on the floor — no dancing pumps for us — we were a tough breed although we had enough sense of rhythm to have danced minuets if they had been on the programme.

Happy days, busy days, and sad ones too as friends were posted away and everything in the process of folding up. The Aussie dances continued and Guy and I spent lots of time together. Then he and two friends were allowed to make a trip into France and Italy, and during that time I was transferred. I wrote to Guy to tell him where I was and wondered if he would surface, and sure enough he did.

It was July 1919, I think, when I had my second leave. Guy was in London awaiting demob. and staying with an aunt in Croydon. I left home on the night train from Newcastle and Guy met me and we had breakfast together, then we proceeded to tour London. Not for us the ancient monuments, nor the romantic Epping Forest or Kew Gardens. We just kept on walking and talking a hundred to the dozen — managed to get food along the route, and finally, after noting that we were in Tottenham we stopped at Pym Park, tried out his new camera, and then trekked back. When my feet were killing me we went into a cinema and saw a western starring Bill Harte whom we had to leave to his fate as I had to join the boat train. There were a number of us going back so there was no place or time for fond farewells. It was the last I saw of Guy for 45 years.

A postscript

We never actually lost complete touch, for my sister, who then closely resembled Meg in appearance, took over the letter-writing which became more frequent when Meg's sister later came to Sydney as a school teacher and stayed with my sister for some time.

I had made up my mind that, on my retirement (in 1962) I would take a trip overseas to visit relatives . and friends in England.

Our sisters had made up their minds (their minds, mark you) that I should call on Meg and both were keeping their fingers and toes crossed to bring this about.

I had been a widower for some years and had some doubts — nay, apprehensions — about the wisdom of this. Nevertheless, the extremity crossings proved potent enough for me to visit Newcastle-on-Tyne in April 1964. Meg and I seemed to take up where we had left off in 1919 and — wait for it! — were married on 22 May 1964.

Guy Oliver

Eileen

Eileen Richards b.1906

26TH January 1911. We were all packed and lined up — six brothers and myself, our pet joey and cocky. Dad surveyed the line-up: Joey and Cocky would have to stay behind with Nana.

Father had migrated to Australia in 1893 from Ireland, going first to Queensland to meet up with his brother Paddy and then two years later settling in Western Australia. Now we were about to depart for Ireland, from Albany, on the White Star liner *Runic*, to have a holiday with our relations.

We arrived in London, spent a week there, proceeded to Dublin, then to County Clare by train — Dad had to hold an umbrella up to keep the rain off us as the roof was leaking. Soon afterwards my brother Jack was born. No wonder Mother was so seasick. It was such a disappointment to me that I was still without a sister that a feeling of real hate came over me. But he was a dear little chap.

Our mother was a very capable and wonderful person but I always felt she was a born boys' mother and, looking back now, my thoughts are still the same. Even my brothers have recently suggested this themselves. I was always expected to be satisfied with my brothers' company and not to feel the need for girlfriends. I was repeatedly told, 'You have your brothers to play with.' Off I would have to toddle to play rugby or cricket with them.

Those were memorable days in Dublin, lots of relations to visit; little enough for Mother to worry about. The boys used to tease me, chasing me with bees or worms or anything they thought would frighten me, then they would admit the poor thing was dead and there would be a funeral with all the ritual and burial.

We all had our jobs to do; washing up was the least favourite and it was not uncommon for whoever's turn it was to make a bee-line for the toilet and a long session, but there was no dodging it. One boy would have to clean the knives on a big emery board with horrible brown powder, another to Brasso the stair rods, and one to black-lead the stove.

One of my jobs was mending socks and shirt tails which made me feel very important as Mother would sit me all comfortably in the glass-house each Saturday afternoon surrounded with baskets of mending, endless socks with plenty of holes in them. In later years I thought it a bit unfair to have had to spend every Saturday like this, but Mother needed the help and I did enjoy it at the time.

Dad returned to Australia after a few months but for some reason we stayed longer. Then in 1914 we were looking forward to returning home and seeing Dad again in the October. Just as if it were yesterday, I can still hear the newspaper boys shouting out 'Stop Press! Stop Press!' on 4 August.

In 1916 Mother and Aunty Susan rented a house together and took in boarders. It didn't work out. I suppose all we kids were partly to blame. We used to make fun of Aunt Susan — she had a very broad Irish accent which amused us and the boys would annoy her by walking across the floor just after she had washed it. But we had some very happy times. We used to go swimming often. We would play tricks on Jack. Once we bought a couple of balloons and the next day, after we were tired of blowing them up, we sent Jack into the shop and told him to say, 'I bought these yesterday and I don't want them now,' hoping we would get our penny back, but poor Jack was chased out.

At Christmas time Mother always dressed up in a Father

Christmas outfit and would be let in the front door by the eldest boy, and walk around the dining room singing 'Adeste Fidelis' and give us a few little presents, then disappear again. The first couple of times I was frightened — something told me it was Mother but I couldn't be sure.

As time went on Jack was the only one still believing in Santa so we thought up the idea of pulling his leg. I dressed in the Santa rigout and my two younger brothers kept Jack out of the way till I knocked on the front door then they told him he was wanted in the drawing room. When he came in I asked him how he liked the bugle I'd given him (I knew he had broken it). He got all shy and upset and said, 'I broke it, Santa'. I sent him to get it and somehow I kidded him that it was working again. He soon woke up that he had been tricked and was furious. (I think he still is.)

As the war years had progressed so Dad's tailoring business in Fremantle had diminished. He was unable to raise enough money to pay all our passages home so even after the war ended we remained in Ireland.

We never gave up hope that each year would be the last we would spend away from home. The 'Trouble' was on in Ireland and it was a constant worry that the boys could be picked up at any time, especially when they were out in the evening and the Curfew was on.

During the 1920s we moved many times as we could not get a long lease for a furnished place. I got a job as a waitress in a café in Dublin. I wasn't paid anything for the first couple of weeks and then ten shillings per week and supply my own uniforms, but still it was a help. I spent a lot of time with my cousins and became very close. I felt at last it was the nearest to having sisters. I know they felt the same towards me.

My eldest brother married, and finally in 1927 Dad arranged for us to return as immigrants on assisted passages. It was sad breaking the ties of all those years and we could hear Pat's coo-ees as we were pulling out from the wharf. And then, after we set sail, we found our cabin luggage had been left behind and we had to manage with what we took on with us.

We were given a great Welcome Home at Fremantle on 4

May 1928 (after seventeen years!), met by Dad and all our uncles and aunts and cousins. But the excitement passed and we realised we had come home to bad times. The Depression had hit and jobs were hard to get. Dad closed the Fremantle shop and his lease had expired on the Hay Street premises. Even travelling the country districts with merchandise only added to the endless numbers of debts on the books. Years later I recall mail arriving with small sums of money sent anonymously, apparently by former debtors as conscience money.

It wasn't long before most of the boys were taking on anything — door-to-door selling of mops, vacuum cleaners, carpet sweepers, etc., even going as far as Kalgoorlie to sell their goods because unemployment hadn't hit there so hard. Work was still available at the mines. But the boys were not earning enough to keep them in shoe leather. Soon they were jumping trains to country towns where they had to report to the police station, get a ration ticket and be told to move out of the area by the next day.

When we were in Ireland I had been keen to go nursing but could never make a start as I always wanted to be free to return to Western Australia. I now applied at Perth Hospital (Royal Perth Hospital) for acceptance as a probationer. There was a waiting list of twelve months. I had to sit for an entrance exam in English and Arithmetic, and began my training in May 1929. I had to provide three uniforms, two pairs of black walking shoes and three pairs of black lisle stockings (the cap was supplied). This outfit was a great strain on the home budget but Mother had learnt to do raffia and cane work and got some orders for baskets. Three of the boys managed to get jobs at the shearing sheds as cooks, roustabouts, anything, during the season.

I made a lot of friends during my training, two very special — Sally an English girl and Gilly who later became my sister-in-law. Our troubles seemed insurmountable at times, the trials and tribulations of junior nurses, but they turned to laughter when we met for a moan and a groan in someone's room at night. The hospital meals were not very enjoyable especially on Sundays — I will never forget the sweets,

always the same, hot custard poured over jelly. Still, we were lucky that we always had a meal. There was so much sadness in the wards amongst the patients, it made me count my blessings.

After my three years training I did some private nursing and then was accepted into Westminster Hospital on Adelaide Terrace. It was a most happy time I spent there — the two matrons knew and understood how to manage staff which included the kitchen and cleaning staff and gardener. A general feeling of goodwill existed at all times.

Two years later, one Saturday morning I went on duty and the patients were all agog with the news that the night sister had got a job on a P. & O. liner and was off to England on Monday. Norah herself was so excited she could hardly talk. One of the nurses had a brother in the P. & O. office who had heard of the vacancy — a radio message came through requiring a sister to be ready to join the ship when she berthed to assist two sisters attending a mental case on board. But on Sunday Norah rang to say she had changed her mind.

Matron Mackie said to me, when I gave her the message, 'There's a chance for you Healy, you are always talking about Ireland.'

It hit me like a bomb, but how could I go? I didn't have two halfpennies to jingle on a tombstone, I remember saying to Mackie, but she kept on — 'You will get paid well, you've got a brother in Ireland and I'll lend you £10. Off you go and your job is here when you get back.'

Well that did it. I immediately thought what a wonderful opportunity to see Pat and Gert once more — they had two children now — and as well, all those dear folk of whom I had grown so fond. I hated to admit it but I did long to return there one day. During the years I had been back in Western Australia I could always sympathise with the immigrants who found it hard to settle. 'A fellow feeling makes one wondrous kind.' I woke Gilly up so she could accompany me home to break the news. This was easier than I thought, although at first it took a little time to convince them that I was not joking. Fortunately Jack was home for a few weeks between jobs up north and he was all agog to help me with preparations next day. Mother got all excited about making me a dressing gown and Dad became quite emotional at the thought of me seeing Pat and bringing back news of his little family.

I slept at the hospital that night to arrange my belongings for Jack to pack. Most important of course was to be at the shipping office in Fremantle at 9 a.m. for an interview with the captain and doctor. Westminster was not far from the Cathedral and after breakfast I went up there to attend Mass as I felt I needed 'some guidance from above'. Then to catch a bus to Fremantle (19 km).

When I look back on that interview I wonder how I kept a straight face as the captain explained the details of my employment. 'You realise there is no pay attached to this agreement?'

Oh yes, I knew that!

'And unlike the two sisters taken on at Sydney, the company will not be responsible for your return to Australia.'

I said I would be all right because I would be glad to visit my brother and other relatives in Ireland.

Everything was in order and I returned to Perth as quickly as I could and got all the business part fixed up and then to the hospital to meet up with Jack and sort out what I was taking with me. The staff had collected ten shillings and some pieces of clothing they thought would be handy for me. We were earning £2 a week so none of us had much to our name. I left a couple of pounds with Mother because I had been helping with the rent.

Jack and I were organised and set out for Fremantle, the others were to meet us on the wharf. On our way from the bus to the ship I thought I had better phone my boyfriend who worked in the country. Jack was getting anxious as it was near sailing time. I got through and had to leave a message. On we ran, and arrived just as they were about to take up the gangway. A quick farewell to everyone, a few parcels thrust at me, including my dressing gown, up the gangway and waving goodbye from the deck when I got a gentle touch on the arm — it was one of the sisters, Beth Sutton. She was so relieved that I had arrived.

Euphemia, our patient, had been a school teacher in England when she had a romance with an Australian holidaying there. She followed him later to Sydney only to find he was married and had a family. She had no money, no friends and nowhere to go. With no hope of employment she became desperate, then had a nervous breakdown and had to be admitted to an institution. At that time shipping companies were held responsible for their passengers if they became a burden on the state during the first three months of landing. The P. & O. company decided to return her to England. They had contacted her nearest relative but apparently there was no co-operation. It was so rough coming through the Bight that Euphie had to be put into a straitjacket as she was so difficult to handle and Beth was seasick.

We were out of Australian waters when Euphemia passed away one night. She was buried at sea and the service was conducted with such reverence it was beautiful to witness and remember. I felt glad that poor Euphemia had not lasted out to get home just to be admitted to an asylum.

The following day Captain Sheepwash (that was his real name) informed me that he and the doctor had decided it was unfair that I was not to get a return passage but if I assisted Doctor during the voyage they would put my case to the P. & O. office in London. Of course I agreed.

On arrival at Tilbury on 18 August there was a letter from Pat waiting for me. I left for Ireland next day. My money just got me there, I travelled steerage.

It was lovely seeing Pat and his two little ones Jim and Fran waiting for me. The first thing he told me was that No. 3 was due in September. Gert was very excited at my return.

A letter from Captain Sheepwash confirmed a return trip available for me and all I had to do was advise a date. I requested the end of October and a ticket was sent to me.

Early September I went to Co. Clare to be with relations before Gert went into hospital. Then I got a telegram from Pat with news of the baby's arrival and a christening arranged for the next Tuesday, 2 October. I returned to Dublin on the Monday and Pat took me to see Gert in the Nursing Home. I was very upset to find that she had her leg elevated and was being treated for thrombosis. Matron assured me that there was no danger and that Doctor was very pleased with her. On Tuesday we picked up the baby, Eileen, and went to the church for the christening, then back to Gert for a little celebration.

Next morning I woke up very depressed after a dream I'd had about some horrible, dirty, creepy crawlies. I couldn't explain it but I got very worried about Gert and wanted to go and see her. Somehow or other there was always some reason why they wanted me to wait; first it was 'wait till afternoon then so-and-so wants to go with you'. Then when afternoon came something else turned up and in the evening Tim and his fiancee had booked to take me to a theatre show in Dublin. After the show I got the bus and Pat met me at Santry. My first question was, 'How was Gert today?' He hadn't been in but rang the Home and was told she was all right. Doctor said she would be up on Friday.

Pat hadn't gone in because Jimmy had been admitted to hospital that day with scarlet fever and he hadn't wanted Gert to be worried so told her Jimmy had a bad cold and he would stay home with him. It was after midnight when we got home, had some supper and talked about Gert's condition. Pat had no idea that it could have been serious. We yarned till about 3 a.m.

I was sound asleep about 6 o'clock when there was a loud banging on the door. I heard Pat going to answer it. It was a policeman to say he had bad news from the nursing home, that all was not well with Gert. As he was about to go he turned and said, 'I'm sorry Mr Healy, but the news is very bad.'

I got Fran up and dressed and off we went. We both knew there was no need to hurry.

Matron said she would care for the baby for a few days till we were sorted out. Pat had many offers of help with the children but it would mean dividing them. I made the decision to cancel my return for the time being and look after the three little ones; Gert would have done that for me. On Monday we brought the baby home.

What a complete change of lifestyle this was for me, baby bottles, formulas to be made up, nappies to be washed, etc. etc., but Eileen was a good baby so that made it easier.

The following Sunday we all went in to get Jimmy. It was a strange experience watching him on the way home. He was excited at seeing his new sister and it was evident he was wondering where his mum was, but not a word. We hadn't even discussed how we should break it to him.

After tea that evening we were sitting round the fire and he crept onto his dad's knee and whispered, 'Daddy, where is Mammy?'

Pat explained to him that she had gone to Heaven and left us the little baby. It is hard to know what goes on in a child's mind but I'm sure he had sensed the truth before he spoke.

After Christmas Jimmy had to start school, that was

another experience for me. The first couple of days went all right then one morning he cried and cried to stay home and I was in tears myself, but thought that he should go. Then all of a sudden he saw a couple of boys from his class and, as if by magic, he bounced off laughing and I was the only one left with tears.

Pat's job took him from home frequently so we went and stayed with Auntie Kit and Uncle Joe for a while. Their daughter Mary Frances and I were good friends and we were able to go to dances and parties around the place. They were happy months.

Meanwhile, Mother and Dad had agreed to take the children for a couple of years till Jim and Fran were ready for boarding school and Pat would be able to arrange something about Eileen. P. & O. sent me a ticket for a first-class cabin, 4-berth, to sail from Tilbury, 16 January. It was a sad farewell leaving Pat on his own, but there was a big gathering to greet us at Fremantle and Eileen was everyone's darling. Mother and Dad were now living on a poultry farm my brother Terry had taken up, 13 km from Perth.

Westminster Hospital had changed hands and I was looking for a job when I saw an ad. in the paper for a policewoman, trained nurse preferred. In May 1936 I became Woman Police Constable Healy No. 1830. The vacancy had occurred due to the retirement of Western Australia's first policewoman, Mrs Dugdale. There had been no increase in these ranks for many years. We were attached to the plain clothes branch and paid the same as the men. We were given files of our own to attend to and a lot of our work concerned missing girls, or going with the CIB or plain clothes on cases dealing with women. We often had to place evicted families while we were on evening duty because Welfare Departments were closed. Sometimes we visited fortune tellers to have our fortunes told then gave evidence in court. Or we tried to catch up on SP betting operations at the racecourse or the trots.

Early in 1938 I met Ted. He had been working on the mines with my brothers and had come to a job in Perth. Last-on-first-off was the order of the day and with so little security we'd made no plans for the future. One morning, in January 1939, he met my bus when I came off duty. His job had finished and he'd decided to go to Darwin as there was plenty of work there. I asked if he was going alone. He said, 'No, I'm getting married.'

Ted started work a couple of days after we arrived in Darwin and two months later a vacancy occurred at the Railway Workshop at what was known as the 'Two and a half' (two and a half miles from town). A house was provided at a nominal rent. These houses had been built in the early days by the Chinese, suitable for the climate with wide verandahs right around. There was a large living room, a kitchen with a woodstove, one bedroom and a bathroom; washtroughs were outside and the toilet a stroll down the back. The verandahs were closed in by wooden shutters, no glass, and when there was the possibility of a storm we would be advised over a loudhailer to batten down. There were all the flying, creeping, crawling insects you could imagine; sandflies undeterred by mosquito netting, glow-worms click-clicking at night shining in the dark; in the morning I'd shake moths out of my slippers, crickets and cockroaches. Ants got into everything.

Dengue fever was one of the trials of Darwin and Ted had a few bouts of it from soon after we arrived. The doctor asked if he'd been having some beers and when Ted said 'No' he advised that it might help if he did. That was a sad day. The doctor didn't know that Ted had been a heavy drinker but hadn't touched it since twelve months before we were married. He came home and asked my opinion and said he was sure he was strong enough to have a few drinks and leave it at that. We decided it was worth trying. It was a few weeks before he gave it up again.

Our baby was due mid-January but at 10 a.m. on 3 December 1939 Dick was born. He was just over four pounds but by 23 December had gained enough weight and we went home. Ted said his friends had been wanting to celebrate but he wouldn't hear of it while I was in hospital. That was the beginning of many more bouts which meant loss of work every now and again.

Once Dick reached his correct birth date he thrived and was a delightful little chap. A lady I had met when we lived in the town used to drop in frequently and loved to watch him in his play pen. She had lost an only child when he was ten years old and said to me, 'Perhaps you will remember me when your boy is ten.'

Darwin was not the right place for anyone with a drinking problem and in December 1940 we left for Sydney where we booked in at the Salvation Army till we could rent a room. Ted was not capable of holding a job and got the idea that at Port Kembla he might be better. We were supposed to be on an afternoon train but Ted was missing when the train pulled out (with our luggage) and we had to sit on the platform till evening, for the next one. When we got to Port Kembla there was no station staff and everything was locked up so we couldn't get our luggage. I suggested we call at the police station as they would advise us where to go. We were in luck. The constable on duty had a home he was not using at the time and drove us there, telling us it was ours till we got settled. He wouldn't discuss payment. We were then down to a few shillings.

In the morning two children knocked on the door and said their mummy had sent them down with some cornflakes and milk and bread and butter in case I wanted something for the baby. The mother came to see me later and said the constable had told her that he thought we didn't have a 'razoo' between us. They were a Jehovah's Witness family and I can never forget what their kindness meant to me.

Ted's father guessed the plight we were in and sent some money occasionally to help us along. We managed to rent a hallway with a double bed from someone near by who was glad of a small payment to help with their rent and we shared the kitchen and conveniences. Ted worked for a while but I was glad when his father in South Australia asked us to come back there to live. Our second child was due in April and this was the end of February.

Ann was born 22 April, with a caul.* I asked to have it kept for me but it had already been discarded. We moved into the house with Ted's father in Gawler. This was where Ted had grown up. It was good to be settled and Ted's aunts and relatives called often. We had plenty of news from Perth.

We had two more children, Veronica and the youngest I named Eileen — but she got called 'B' — she was a real sticky beak and pushed in everywhere saying, 'B! B!' (probably meant 'me').

Once I got to know the neighbours it made such a difference to life. Of course it was difficult to get many necessities during the war but it was handy to be able to swap coupons. In Adelaide for shopping I always kept my eyes open for queues. That was a sure sign that something in short supply had arrived but until you were almost at the counter few of us knew what we were queueing for. Very often, whatever it was, had been sold out before your turn came. Once I was lucky and got some elastic.

We had our ups and downs in Gawler but when Ted was working everything was bright and we were very proud of our little family. It was a truly happy home, neither of us drew a line as to what each should do, we just worked like a team.

There were the bad times which I dislike referring to, but I will just say it was nothing short of hell. Anyone who has lived with an alcoholic will know what I mean. Then the sun would shine again and we would sit and talk things over. Ted would vow and declare that never ever could he treat me and the children like that again. He'd make plans the next day for getting a new job and I'd give him the money (sometimes just the little I had). It probably sounds as though I was very gullible, but it was a matter of trust and if I couldn't bring myself to trust him, what could I expect?

---

* A membrane sometimes enclosing a child's head at birth (O.E.D.). A child born with a caul would be lucky and must never part with it (Eileen's mother told her). In early times a captain would not take out to sea without one and would pay a good price if anybody would part with one.

The next day would seem endless, hour after hour I'd watch down the road as people were coming from the train, then some time during the night back he'd come and all the good intentions were down the drain. Fortunately, when Grandpa became an invalid his brother advised him that he should pay his pension to me.

Grandpa died towards the end of 1948. He had left the house to Ted and me. Unknown to me, Ted went straight to the solicitor to make his share over to me, explaining that in his hands the money would not provide a home.

Ted had often talked of returning to the West and after Christmas 1948 he wrote to the Railway Workshop in Midland and he was given an appointment for an interview, so we decided to sell. We returned to Perth in February and immediately put our name down for state housing. Meanwhile Mother and Dad put us up. It was lovely to see them all again. Jimmy and Fran were working, Eileen was still at school. She had grown very tall and had big brown eyes like her mother. Pat had married again but Molly didn't want to come to Australia and the children didn't want to go back to Ireland.

We were hoping that the Housing Commission would give us a flat in the old Air Force camp down the end of the street from Mother because the children had started school close by. One of these flats became vacant and next day I got word that they had a place for us and to go in and get the key. I nearly died when they told me we were going way out to Guildford, another camp they were using. I was told they had made enquiries and had formed the opinion that my husband was not reliable enough to be allowed the Wembley flat. It just stunned me that anyone behind a counter could be responsible for making that decision to the detriment of a family.

Out we went and settled in. It meant a change of school again and being right away from friends and relations.

It was August when we moved to Guildford. (The Guildford flat had become vacant due to a plane that crashed shortly after takeoff and landed right outside our place, killing all eighteen people aboard. The occupants of the house were shocked and refused to stay there any longer.) Michael and Gilly's son Peter was having his ninth birthday in October. They decided to make it a picnic day at Serpentine Weir. Michael was taking his car and a friend of his taking a utility. On 16 October they called at our place about 11 a.m. to pick up our crowd and belongings. Stan's utility got bogged where the plane had come down.

It was a beautiful day for a picnic and the children were having a wonderful time. Gilly had prepared all sorts of goodies. The three boys, Peter, Anthony and Dick, decided they would stroll over to the weir while Gilly and I were getting the sweets dished up.

That is the last time I saw Dick alive.

In a short while the other boys came back. When I looked up and saw only two, I knew something had happened. They said he had slipped in and that there were lifesavers picnicking nearby who were trying to find him. We all rushed over, but there was no sign of him.

The police came and next morning they found him wedged between rocks.

He would have been ten in December.

Dorothy

Dorothy Enid Ross b.1899

THE most painful memory of my childhood concerns my last days at kindergarten when I was nearly seven. I wasn't happy at this private pre-school, self-conscious that my dresses were not as dainty as the other girls'. These girls were not really friendly and any popularity I might have had I lost by stealing a cake (on two separate occasions) from two different lunch baskets.

I was discovered (I don't know how) and after that no-one was allowed to speak to me. For good measure I was kept in after school. Mother came looking for me and heard the whole story, though not in my hearing. My punishment was not yet over.

Mother was a strict Presbyterian then and believed in 'Spare the rod and spoil the child'. I was ordered to strip naked when we reached home and was thrashed with a leather strap on my bare bottom and round the legs as I ran up and down the passageway trying to escape. As the eldest child this beating was a blow to my pride. More was to come. My father, whom I loved dearly, did not speak to me for a fortnight.

I never stole another thing in my life, except from the household larder and became almost pathologically honest. I must have had a craving for sweet things because I would raid the pantry at home when dates came in the grocery delivery. And Mother, who had health plans for us all, gave us very little sugar on our porridge and never made cakes, either because she was too busy to make them or was anxious to preserve our teeth.

Although she believed so strongly in discipline, Mother was an idealist. The fact that I was called Dorothy (meaning 'gift of God') and Enid (meaning 'soul') chosen from 'Idylls of the King' by Tennyson, seems to indicate she wanted me to be perfect in body, mind and soul.

In 1899 the beachline where our home was in South Perth would not have been opened up and there was most likely a thick fringe of bushland through which a pathway had been cleared by residents who occasionally went for a swim. Mother, at any rate, found a secluded spot where she sunbaked in the nude for a short period each day until the onset of the cool autumn weather. In addition to ensuring the good health of her baby, she also studied her Bible and read Tennyson, Ruskin and Emerson among others, so that some of the concentrated cultivation of her own mind might reach mine and ensure a taste for reading and good literature.

Slang and bad language of any kind was prohibited in our family; no crude jokes were ever told and seldom did we hear any in our circles. I heard the 'facts of life' first from friends at school, and quite disbelieved them for some time until Mother gave me an attractive little book on the subject to read. We never had a discussion about it; it was tied up delicately with religion which was another delicate subject, notwithstanding our knowledge of Bible stories.

Both parents observed the rule about bad language although I occasionally heard an explosive 'Blast!' when Father thought we were well out of the way. If we called one another a 'fool' at any time, Scripture was quoted and an eternity promised in hell. Satan and hellfire were constantly used in quelling our normal reactions to one another and to the daily problems of life. We were not allowed to quarrel, use our fists or pull each other's hair. No wonder that a young nurse during our father's last illness told me she had never met a family before who were so polite to each other.

Dorothy with grandmother and brother

About the age of twelve I developed an abnormal religious sense. If we had been Roman Catholic I would have considered becoming a nun. Life was becoming more difficult. With the passage of years and four children to cope with, plus the onset of asthma in her early forties, Mother did not seem to manage so well, always seemed in a bad humour and nagged too much. I had overheard a neighbour say to Mother, 'Why don't you get that great lump of a girl to do a bit of work for a change?' I was staggered, having been under the impression I did nothing else but work once we were home from school and during the weekends. I once said to Murray, 'Mother said I could come out to play for five minutes. Isn't she kind?' I was not in a sarcastic mood — it was a genuine tribute. In later years my sisters often accused me of having a sarcastic sense of humour, and it shocked me every time.

Although I was kept busy, there did not seem to be any change in the general appearance of the home. I probably added to the disorder. Despite numbers of shelves and cupboards in the house, a walk-in pantry, a walk-in linen cupboard, a dressing room off a large bedroom — all planned by herself — Mother did not seem capable of making use of them to devise a system of orderly house-keeping. She was always mislaying things and I was detailed to find them. I know that I left shelves and drawers in worse disorder than I found them. Half the time I wasn't sure what I was looking for, and dark thoughts of running away from home were churning around with feelings of hatred for Mother and resentment against my hard lot. I would not have recognised what I was looking for in that state of mind. It was always a relief to see the lengthening shadow of the fence and its burden of convolvulus, on our western side. It meant our father would soon be home and the general temperature of the home restored to normal.

I have written the foregoing with the most loving respect for Mother at this time. I realise that organisation in the home was not one of her gifts. I have inherited a great deal from her (and God who provides all gifts), and I also have inherited her lack of order in housekeeping. Perhaps a good housekeeper is born, just as a great singer or artist or poet is born. The only gift I have ever envied, really envied, is that ability of a good, tidy, spotlessly clean housekeeper. Life is much simpler if you are always ready for visitors.

It was at this difficult time that I converted the dressing room off the bedroom I shared with my sister, into a chapel. I had been given a New Testament on my eighth birthday, and I had two nice little pictures, one of Jesus at prayer in Gethsemane and the other of young Samuel hearing his first call from God. These and a few other small ornaments I thought suitable for a chapel were set out neatly on the lower shelf. One of the numerous chairs in the house became my pew. Here I read my Testament, and prepared lists of people to pray for and things such as forgiveness and help, banishment of faults, the sick and the sorrowful. It sounds rather pathetic, but I believe it helped me through that troubled period of life felt by most early-teenagers.

I like to recall the grace and gentility of those days before the First World War. In South Perth especially, a suburb cut off from the capital by river, and not then reachable by any means other than ferryboat (unless one hired a cab to bring you over the Causeway, which would have been unthinkable, if not prohibitive financially), the relaxed weekend somehow had a familial quality. During the weekends it was customary for just about every man in the vicinity of the Spa Baths at the Zoological Gardens to stroll leisurely in his bathrobe, towel over his arm, in the direction of the Spa entrance. It was a different entrance on Labouchere Road and visitors to the Zoo and to the Spa could not be mistaken.

Another custom was for entire families already dressed in Sunday best for church service, to go for a stroll round the suburb on Sunday afternoons: up and down the tributary streets observing the progress of gardens, stopping for a brief chat here and there, sometimes accepting an invitation to 'come in for a cup of tea', sometimes joined by a passing friend also on tour. I was very interested in those girls round my own age whose voile blouses were so finely woven that every detail of embroidery or lace on their underwear was visible. In fact it was the fashionable objective of the moment: the delectable camisole was more important than the blouse or bodice.

I was interested, too, as I was growing up, in the number of girls allowed to go walking with their boyfriends, also dressed in the fashion of the moment. It was with a little envy perhaps that I once remarked to Mother, 'So-and-so has a different boyfriend every Sunday!' No secrets in the suburbs in those days. We knew every woman who was divorced, and of course she was shunned. We suspected every well-dressed single woman of being a barmaid: although we did not know why it was not considered a good profession for a woman at that time, we accepted the consensus of opinion.

The death of our parents within six months of each other in August 1930 and February 1931 was the hardest ordeal we'd had to bear till then. Our father was certainly a victim of the Depression: he died a bankrupt. Mother had not known that this was an actual possibility, but she was no fool and we found quite a cache of £5 notes in the bottom of one of her trunks after she died.

In the evening after her funeral Father took Nancy and myself to the local picture show. There were not many people there and I at least was glad about this, for it was not accepted conduct of a newly bereaved family to seek enter-tainment. We did not go into black, either, but this did not bother me. By this time I had discovered we were 'free thinkers', although we did not belong to any organisation of that name. We just went on living as normally as possible, however much we felt our loss. Father was very interested in spiritualism and at the time of his own death I realised the reasoning behind our visit to the picture show.

We were all there except Murray when Father died. The daily help at this time was a young single woman we had engaged ourselves. On the day of Father's death we all gathered round his bed, including the young woman. She knelt and gazed into his face as though she were chief mourner among those present. I suppose as the eldest of the family I should have gently led her from the room — but that was one of the failures of my sheltered upbringing. At thirty-one I was not even capable of thinking I should do anything.

We later heard that our daily help was pregnant when she came to us a few weeks before, and it was suggested to us that she may have been hoping a sight of death would induce a miscarriage. If that was the case, only her plan miscarried, but on the day of Father's funeral she was on hand to create a minor miracle with two fish, providing a beautiful fish pie for a number of visitors who came to cheer us.

Chief among these was one of Father's friends, an old lady, clairvoyant and a member of the Spiritualist Church of Perth. She had joined us to create a happy atmosphere, not only for us but for the departed spirit of our father. She knew all he had endured through the last few years and probably of his imminent bankruptcy, and she wished to ensure that

110

we did not keep his spirit earthbound by grief and tears. That lunch hour was one of the brightest in memory, but I cannot recall a word of how she did it. But she was of Irish descent, and the Irish can always make you laugh when they want to.

I had shed all the tears I had in my heart when Mother died (and no doubt kept her earthbound). Our clairvoyant friend had not warned us of the dangers of grief on that occasion. Mother was not interested in spiritualism but drawn more to the healing aspects of Christian Science.

Ivy

Ivy Burke b.1904

I was born at Eagle Point in Victoria, a silt jetty about eight miles (13 km) long between Lake King and the Mitchell River. I remember clearly my fifth birthday when I had on a bright red pinafore with white spots and a frill round the armhole, and some little girls put me in a cart my father had made out of a fish box, wheels and two board shafts. They took me along the lake which was the bottom of our backyard. There were lots of rushes, ti-tree, boobialla and other trees along the edge of the lake, also a lot of pink pigface, little white daisies and a small purple flower. The lake had lots of swans, ducks, coots, dabchicks, grebe and other birds on it. It was quite shallow and sandy at the edge but gradually got deeper as you waded out.

At the party there were hundreds-and-thousands on bread and butter and little cakes, and I got a little cup and saucer from one girl and I still have it.

My father had ten acres of land he was buying from the Closer Settlement Board. When I first remember, he grew vegetables and there was a fruit orchard of apples and apricots. He had a covered-in four-wheel cart and horse and used to hawk produce round Bairnsdale, our nearest town. My mother used to go with him and take me and my little brother and when he sold things and got some money she bought groceries and meat for the week. We always had a

7 lb bag of flaked oats which we had for breakfast every morning. We also had hens and ducks and a cow.

My father was always late no matter what he did. He was an Englishman and an avid reader half the night and got up late. Never started his work till 8 or 9 o'clock and milked in the dark. Never started his vegetable round till everyone else was coming home. In the end he lost his customers and just worked the land, grew peas, beans and potatoes and so on and sent them to market in the city most times. He never sprayed the fruit trees and he got a notice to grub out the apples as the moth spread to other farms.

I don't remember having many toys or good clothes, only what my mother made on a hand sewing-machine. She made her own jam, sauce and soap when she had enough fat. When we ran out of meat, which was often, my father shot a duck or trapped a rabbit.

The house was weatherboard and never painted; four rooms, a back and front door, no passage, no ceiling in the kitchen and hessian lining in the back bedroom, with paper and hessian in the other two rooms. There was a colonial stove in the kitchen until after I got married and an open fireplace in the 'front room' (as we called it). This was the only room with lino on the floor; it had a sofa in it and a table in the middle on which stood a very tall kerosene lamp with a lovely pink fluted glass shade which was a wedding present to my mother. There was a small table in one corner with a cruet on it and a biscuit barrel with red and white painted design.

The kitchen had table and chairs, wooden, no lino on the floor for years; a long couch was set near the wall and there was a big tall dresser with muslin curtains hanging down the front, and another red-painted safe with zinc-wire set in both ends. Above the safe, set on a board fastened to the wall were six cowhorns where you hung your hats, caps, etc., which everyone wore in those days.

The front bedroom had a brass bed with white bed hangings with hairpin lace that my mother had made for her glory box, also pillow shams (decorative covers) of lovely white linen, handworked. The wardrobe was a corner one with curtains down the front and a nice four-drawer dressing-table with two small drawers on the top and a swing mirror. I slept in an iron cot beside my mother when my brother came along two years later. My mother fed us all on the breast till we were over a year old and we slept between Mum and Dad.

When the following brother came along I went into the back bedroom with an iron bed and a palliasse that contained straw packed tight and buttoned down. It was in two halves and was very hard but later we had a flock mattress on top of it. Lots of times we had no proper blankets but were never cold as Mother cut out old woollen overcoats and lined them with sacking and any other cotton material she could get hold of.

In each room there was only one small window with six small panes of glass in two frames. We often had cardboard in one pair which would get broken sometimes and it would be weeks before my father got around to putting another pane in. He was no handyman about the home. But he loved animals, especially horses which he always seemed to have a few of. Before I went to school I learned to ride a pony but was very nervous.

We used to have pet lambs. We had no sheep but on the other side of the river there were lots of sheep, and lambs used to fall down the bank and could not get up again so Dad used to row a boat over and bring them home and warm them up and bottle feed them, or I did, when I got older. We used to put a collar around their necks and chain and tether them out to feed and later sell them to the baker that came round with a horse and cart from Paynesville. He used to kill and eat them but we hated the thought after they had been pets.

My mother told me that when I was a bit over two years old and my brother six weeks, we got whooping cough and were never taken to a doctor which was eight miles away and Dad didn't believe in doctors anyway. It left both of us with asthma and I suffered with it all my life.

Some time before I was six I got lots of boils in my crutch and could not walk. Mother put poultices on them, very hot,

Ivy with brothers Roy and Clement

and I cried and so did she. I was on a couch in the kitchen — in the end they sent me to an aunt in Glenferrie to see if the change would do me good. It cured the boils but I got yellow jaundice, had some teeth out, also went to another aunt in Richmond and fell and broke my arm at the elbow. I was taken to St Vincent's in the tram and they set it, put it in a splint and bound it around with a sticky bandage and after a while they opened it up and peeled the sticky off also all the hairs and sometimes skin so I did not like going. But it set well and I had to carry weights to make it strong and straight and I've never had any trouble with it.

When I went home after about three months, all pale and thin, my mother hardly knew me, but I soon got brown again and had to start school which was a mile along the river, on a dirt road, a one-room school with residence built on the side, lots of water tanks, pine trees, and a garden in front, gravel round the door, a pony paddock at the back and a big garden plot at the side where the boys learned to grow vegetables. We had a small shelter shed to eat our lunch in, about twenty of us.

The district has changed so much since then. There were so many water birds and many others nesting in the bushes and trees — lots of animals such as hares, rabbits, bandicoots, foxes, porcupines, water rats, to mention a few.

Lake King, or Eagle Point Bay, which was at the back of our house was teeming with all sorts of fish. The sailing boats came over from Paynesville dragging a dinghy. The men ran their seine net around, left it for a while, then hand-hauled it in. Sometimes with so many garfish they could not take them all home in their boats so they cut ti-tree poles and ran a bag net around them and came back for them later.

I often took them down a billy of tea and they would carry me out to the boat and sit me on deck to watch. When I went home they gave me lots of fish and told me to hunt the seagulls away from the ones they left behind. Sometimes dolphins came through Lakes Entrance (Cunningham, then) and big schools of them used to leap right out of the water. The fishermen used to try to drive them out, they also got big conger eels in their nets and killed them with a tommy-axe then threw them overboard. They floated to the bank and our dogs used to love to roll in them, and did they smell.

Where we lived, about four miles from the mouth of the Mitchell, there were only nine houses and a shipbuilding slip right at the mouth where they built small boats and did repairs for quite a few years. There are still a few old barges there today and an odd fisherman's hut, but most of the houses are long since gone. They have stopped selling the land and are trying to make it a sanctuary. Our old home has been made over and called 'The Two Bells'.

My brother took over the farm and quite a few others over the years as no one could make a living on such small blocks. He sold the land in building blocks after my father died as the lake washed away acres of it because all the trees, rushes, etc. had been cut down or washed away with the rough weather. Also the river bank was being washed away by the boats that came up to Bairnsdale with cargo from

Melbourne twice a week, and every day a passenger boat from Cunningham as well as motor launches, and the cows used to eat the rushes and made places to go down to drink and the road got so narrow, a cart or car could not get along so they took a piece of your land to widen it. Today the rushes have grown back and no animals around, no big steamers come up and there are some very nice houses built all along.

The old school was shifted a few miles further up on the Paynesville road before I left and it was then about three miles to go. Lots of times I walked, then I had a pony and at dinnertime took it to a waterhole in the park for a drink and brought cows and sometimes horses to drink at night as the river was sometimes salty if an easterly wind blew. Other times after school I would cut maize and throw it over the fence for the cows and eat some of the young corn as we got hungry after a cut lunch of stale bread and jam and sometimes beef dripping which we liked. We took some corn home to cook in front of the stove or in a pot of soup. Dad used to tell us we did the cows out of the best part.

At odd times I used to handmilk which I hated so I fed fowls, poddies, pigs, etc. before helping Mother with the tea. There were three boys after me, then a sister born when I was ten and another when I was fourteen. I worked hard on the farm for a girl, planted potatoes in a furrow behind my father drawing the horse with my back bent for hours, picked peas, beans, maize, etc. The hardest was hauling a

Chaffcutting in Gippsland

kerosene tin of water out of the river and tipping it into a trough for the horses to drink. And did they drink! I was lucky to get a penny when I went to Bairnsdale to buy some broken biscuits and pick out the ones with lolly icing on.

We all wore heavy boots. I remember my first pair of shoes. I went to stay with friends at Lindenow and helped pick peas and they bought me shoes for best. We got very little from Father Christmas, perhaps one small toy then a few raisins in a little bag and a small bottle with hundreds-and-thousands in it, a paper whistle — but I don't remember being unhappy as no-one else got very much more. And we got a few secondhand toys when my aunts or cousins came to visit from the city at holiday time. They enjoyed the swimming in the lake and river with us — we also had an old boat in the river and a home-made raft made out of willow logs brought down in the floods, with boards nailed across.

In later years we had neighbours with a motor boat and they took us up the Tambo and Nicholson rivers for picnics in the summer time and we fished with ti-tree poles and cord lines, just a hook and sinker, and caught lots of fish. Shoals of mullet came up the river and we just dangled the line in and caught hundreds. We had them cooked every way, and Mother opened them up flat and dried them in the sun for later. So it was not always a bad life with a pony to ride or horse to drive in a buggy.

Sometimes the tanks would almost dry out and we used to load up the spring cart with tubs, kerosene tins and rope lines and drive about six miles to Forge Creek to do the washing; dip water out of the creek, light a fire and boil the whites in a tin and drive home very tired. No wonder my poor mother was never very well. She had a stomach ulcer and died with kidney disease.

When I left school I picked peas and beans for people around, also hops in season — walked three miles with others, then rowed across the river and picked hops into a bin all day in the sun. Earned about three to four shillings a day while it lasted. That was the only way to get a few clothes, shoes, etc.

Ivy with pillion rider, around 1919

There used to be send-offs for the local soldiers in the First World War. They had a dance in the local school and served supper. We children enjoyed it and the little ones slept at the back. We had an accordion and concertina for music and put sawdust and candlegrease on the floor to make it slippery. They did the set-dances and all the lovely old waltzes. Then the Military Twostep came in. We drove home at all hours, with a lantern.

When I was about sixteen I worked at Lindenow for a time, cooking and cleaning. Now and again I rode a pony about 12 miles home for the weekend, and got up early on the Monday morning and rode back and the frost was thick on the bridges. I used to take the men's afternoon tea down the flat where they were picking maize and ride up the rows and they were over the pony's head. I got ten shillings a week and my keep. When I went into service I got twenty-five shillings a week and keep, half day off a week and every second Sunday a half day. I worked with this family in Box Hill for quite a few years. A week off once a year I went home to the farm in Gippsland.

In 1927 I got married, twenty-three years old. Work was very hard to get even then. My husband, Rob, was a plumber, also his brother, and they followed up any work they could get. We rented a small house in Essendon and had basic new furniture that my husband paid off. He mostly worked for big contractors and when one job was finished he found it hard to get another. He used to get up early for a paper and go to jobs and often there would be so many there that they used to draw lots, then go on to another one and often came home tired out and no job. We kept going for a little over twelve months when he met with an accident to his knee at work, put a cartilage out and had to rest up. I think we got about thirty shillings a week till he had it operated on, then they gave us £6 to sign off. He had to get out of bed for me to get in for my first baby which I had at home. As he had a stiff leg and could not walk we came to my father's home in Gippsland and they looked after us till he could get a bit of pea and bean picking or whatever.

After a few months his brother sent for him as he landed a big job in Griffith NSW and his other brother lived there. So we borrowed the fare and went to live with them for about six months till work ran out and they did odd jobs. Then they landed another big job for the same contractor, a new hotel in Hillston and we shifted up there and rented two rooms and use of kitchen.

I used to get so lonely as I knew no-one and it seemed so far from home and friends, and I was expecting again. Work was running out, and being a small country town not much hope of finding any, even on stations, by this time. So I wrote home and told them the situation we were in and my father had an empty house which he said we could move into. We knew we could get milk off them for the two children — I had a daughter six weeks old. When we shifted, it took us about a week to get there. We had acquired an old wine truck with solid tyres. It took a wire mattress in the back and we camped along the way. As it was July it was very cold at night and we had to light camp fires to warm bottles and cook whatever we could afford. We had sold our little furniture before we left and that's all the money we had.

We could not camp near bridges as there were so many swagmen on the way looking for work or whatever they could find to live on. Some of them were almost in rags and so thin. We ourselves never went really hungry though the food we had was not the best. I remember one place we camped, a man in a truck gave us quite a lot of apples he couldn't sell, so I stewed some for us and our little boy, and we ate a lot raw which was good for us.

We had lots of truck troubles along the way as there were a lot of dirt roads, very rough. My husband was a very good handyman and managed to repair and make do with things. At last we arrived, very tired, and shifted into an old weatherboard house on the Mitchell river, about a mile from my parents' place. There were some old beds, a table, a few old chairs, etc. It was built upon high stumps with four steps back and front and had a hardwood floor with big cracks in it. When the wind blew it was very cold and the roof leaked in lots of places and windows were broken, but there was plenty of room and it was home to us for quite a while. There was lots of space for the children to play and we soon had a veg. garden and my husband's mother gave us six hens. She was on the old age pension and could not help us much.

My husband rode a bike for miles around the country trying to get tanks to make or any sort of plumbing, which at odd times he did, but making a tank by hand was hard work. I used to get inside when he had it rounded off and hold an old flat iron for him to rivet it together.

Nearly every evening he would set a rabbit trap as we could not afford much meat. Sometimes we would sell a pair in Bairnsdale for sixpence each. We saved the skins and sold them to a tanner for a few pence a pound. We also went fishing, often caught a lot and cooked them in different ways. At first, having no stove, we cooked on the open fire, but later we were given an old worn-out one and my husband put a new iron in the back and bricked it in for me which was much easier. Before that I had to go to my mother's place to bake a cake or pie in her wood stove as she only had a colonial oven for years till my husband put a stove in for her. He also put a tap inside from a tank and she did not have to go down steps and outside to fill the kettle. Thank the Lord my husband was a handyman. He could do almost any job and that's how we earned our rent, milk and any other thing that we got from my father, who was no good with tools but looked after his animals well.

My brothers had motor bikes and took Rob with them when they went pea or bean picking and we got some for ourselves. Also we could pick up small potatoes, chats they called them, that they could not sell. Friends and neighbours in the country gave away any surplus fruit they had and I learned to make jam, etc. before I left home. We had no clear bottles so we collected beer bottles and Rob made an iron to fit over the neck and you made it hot, held it for a time, then dipped the bottle in water and the top fell off. When you filled them with jam you pasted down the top with brown paper and starch or flour paste.

Rob learned to half-sole our shoes. He got old leather saddle flaps from home and soaked them, and in the end he could do a good job. I used to buy sugar bags for threepence each, wash them and make pinnies for my little girl and myself. They looked nice bound around with something bright and I used 25 lb flour bags to line my son's pants that I cut from the leg of my brothers' worn-out ones. I had a machine which helped a lot to patch and mend as everyone did in those days. I still had sheets from my glory box and I made rugs out of old coats and things, whatever I could scrounge, and lined them with hessian chaff bags. They called them 'woggers', and they kept us warm.

I used to walk up to my father's place once a week with the two children. I had an old antique pram and we would drive into Bairnsdale and get a few groceries, mostly flour, sugar, rice, tea and flaked oatmeal as we always had porridge in the mornings. Sometimes we could afford a bit of meat but as there were no fridges then we had to get a bit of corn beef to last out the week. The baker came in a cart twice a week, bread was about fourpence or sixpence a loaf. If we ran out I made a scone loaf in the oven so we were well off compared with a lot of people in the city.

I would hate my family to go through what we did as I

don't think they could cope like us. Those days no-one had much to start with and were brought up the hard way, learning to manage with what they could get and not wasting a thing. Even now I can't waste anything, though I love my own home and can afford comforts and a holiday every year. I am sure it all hastened my husband's death as he worked so hard to rear his family and give them a better education and life than he had. He was a very good husband. He died in 1973, aged seventy-four, and was brave till the last.

I keep reasonably well, but have had asthma all my life. These days the Ventolin Inhaler helps me when I over-exert myself. Also I have arthritis in the lower back but take Brufin every day and it keeps it in check but after gardening, which I love, it plays up a bit. I only have to take one blood pressure tablet a day so I am doing well as I play croquet two days a week if the weather is good. On Tuesdays and Fridays I go to the Elderly Citizens Club for a hot meal and play cards in the afternoon. Some Sundays I go to the Uniting Church and one of my children's families often come to see me in the afternoon.

Wednesdays I like to do a bit of gardening. I have a small vegetable garden, lots of tomatoes to make relish to bottle and give away. Also beans carrots and silverbeet, picked my last butternut today. I still make my own jam, etc. and don't ever remember buying any. I have a few fruit trees loganberry bushes and friends give me fruit. I have quite a few pot plants around the porch at the back.

I have a son and three daughters they have sixteen children between them and there are eight great grandchildren. All the single ones are working and all healthy so I am a very lucky person as I have all the comforts I need — not used to the grand life.

I had a very loving and caring husband and worked for all I have now only wish that he could have lived longer to enjoy it but would not wish him back to suffer. I nursed him at home quite a few months, he has been gone now over ten years. I get a bit lonely at night but have television, and knit and crochet but my hearing is failing badly. I have an aid but cannot hear very well, can't walk so far or fast or sleep so well but thank God for a long life.

Thora

Thora S. Shoesmith b.1903

ALL my early memories are of our (rented) home in Hope Street, South Yarra. Mother and Father first lived in Canterbury Road, Toorak: they were there in 1901 as sewerage was being installed, and the day Queen Victoria died the men told Mother, 'We can't work today, mum, the Queen's dead.'

Our house in Hope Street was the first of four terrace houses with a slightly larger back yard than our three neighbours. We always had a canvas hammock, made at sea by my father, in the yard and this was a great attraction to nearby children. We also had a deck chair, frame made by 'Chips' (the carpenter on board ship) and canvas cover made by Father with his neat stitching. I can see him now, canvas held over a large palm, sewing with a large curved needle and twine and a piece of beeswax handy.

The house was single-fronted, had a narrow strip of garden in front, a verandah and a gas box. One entered the front door into a passage off which were three rooms to the right. The front room, always so-called, was my parents' bedroom, the middle one a skylight room and rather dark, the third a sitting room which had a window at the side. The living room was at the end of the passage. This had a fireplace. One had to go through this room to the kitchen-wash-house-cum-bathroom: the stove, copper, troughs and bath were all in together. The tin bath my mother used to paint white and the paint continually peeled off with the hot water.

The house had wallpaper, most of it revolting, which put me off wallpaper for life. The horrible brownish paper used to give me nightmares as a child; I suffered a lot from headaches (was always sick inside cable trams), and can remember many a time when the pattern of the paper seemed to rise up and quell me. When Father's ship was 'on the Indian run' he used to bring home yards and yards of red or green cotton holland with which Mother covered just about everything in the house, including my two brothers and me. I can recall lying on the old sofa with its red cotton cover, my head aching, wallpaper rebounding, and my inner self floating above my body.

I think Karl and I shared the skylight room; Herman, who contracted poliomyelitis when he was three, slept out on the front verandah, and Axel when he arrived was in the front room with Mother, and Father when he was home. As Karl went off to the First World War when he was eighteen and I thirteen, I don't suppose there were any embarrassing moments.

At the Domain Road end, Hope Street is narrow, but halfway to Toorak Road it broadens out, and in my day was cobbled. At the bend where it widens, people named Morrison had a dairy with great fearsome cows. Or was it only one cow? The Mutual Store (Flinders Street) had stables in Millswyn Street, a short way up a lane. (This part of South Yarra was honeycombed with lanes.) The stables were of a considerable size with the most delicious odour of horses and hay; the land extended right to Domain Road behind the Millswyn Street houses, fenced with hoardings; nowadays there are flats on the site.

On the opposite corner of this lane was the house where I first attended a little dame school. It was run by Miss F. M. Trice. I was five and a half and could not have been properly house-trained as I remember a pool on the floor on my first day. About a dozen or fifteen pupils, we were taught to spell and add up which is more than a lot of children can do today.

Thora, Karl and Herman

Mother paid a shilling a week, and when Herman started it was 1s 6d for the two of us. In all I was there nearly three years and then I think Miss Trice must have been forced to relinquish because of health regulations. But we not only learned to read and write, we did craft work with coloured paper and energetic exercises with dumb-bells and wooden clubs. Miss Florence May Trice died only recently (1982) in her 103rd year.

We were indeed fortunate as children to live where we did, the Domain and Botanical Gardens on one side of us and Fawkner Park on the other. The Domain then was an uncultivated area of long grass and wildflowers, of many Moreton Bay Fig trees and pine trees whose delicate tiny nuts were a joy to discover and crack with great patience. It took so many nuts to make a handful of the small kernels — was it better to eat them one by one as cracked, or save them up until a number made a mouthful?

We knew just about every inch of the Gardens (never called Botanical by us), picnicking during holidays or weekends, playing hide-and-seek in the fernery, in and out the windows of the summer houses, or feeding the ducks,

In the Botanical Gardens, 1913. Thora third from left

eels and swans. The flowers did not mean much to us, we were not at all interested in the Australian section, but we loved the lakes, particularly the small one when the water lilies were in bloom. The Oak Lawn, though a long way from the teahouse, was always cool in summer. Some parts of the Gardens seemed a bit sinister to us and we did not often go over to the river side near the Tan where the horses were ridden. Once when the large lake was drained, we walked across the cracked muddy bed from one side to the other. Itinerant photographers took our photo sometimes, and once with Lady Someone-or-other sketching — she was probably from Government House.

We often rode by cable tram to Town, and I recall the Old Colonists homes along St Kilda Road, with the elderly people sitting outside: and also the thrill of travelling by horse tram to the zoo. Other hazy shadows in my mind are of a kind of water chute somewhere in St Kilda Road opposite the present Music Bowl. This was confirmed by an article in Melbourne's *Age*, 25 October 1974, in which was described a giant water chute at Princes Court Amusement Park, now the site of the Melbourne Arts Centre. The same site from

127

1880 onwards was used regularly by circuses. Early in the century it contained the Saucer Track skating rink and Café Chantant open-air theatre, followed by a succession of dance halls the last being the Trocadero, popular rendezvous during the Second World War. And workmen digging the Arts Centre foundations dug up evidence of an even earlier period of Melbourne's history — the remains of ancient bottles and brickbats. Originally a swamp, it was used by Melbourne as a rubbish tip.

My brother Karl used to go yabbying in Albert Park Lake, where nearby we found mushrooms and once we walked over to South Melbourne market with other kids and a billycart in tow — a hell of a long walk it must have been.

My father was Swedish, born in 1868, his father being a schoolmaster and also church organist. He was tall and dark and handsome, very well built, and in my childhood had a moustache, smoked a pipe, and wore a bowler hat when ashore. His navy-blue suits were always made double breasted with little round eyelets where his gold seafaring buttons could be switched to black ones when ashore. He was with McIlwraiths for thirty-four years and when they had the Indian run he wore beautiful white duck suits which I would collect from Mrs Jorgensen after laundering.

We were always very proud of our Swedish father and his being 'different'. We all had Swedish names and felt a cut above some of the neighbouring children whose fathers worked in tobacco or jam factories; we skited about our father being chief officer in a ship.

My mother was born and bred in Sydney, and to her there was no place like it. She took Herman and me to Sydney by sea in 1911. (Where was Karl?) She hated the sea and must have been the world's worst sailor, spending all the time in her bunk. Children's meal times were separate from adults' and I can remember Herman and I going down for a meal and Herman was sick on the stairs. I pretended he did not belong to me.

Father never came home from sea empty-handed, always laden with presents and books for us all. Sometimes they

were most preposterous things like sea-shell birds stuck together with glue which all fell to pieces in the hot weather. And my mother got tired of asking Father to get Chips to make furniture or stools, etc. for the house, as they were always so damn heavy no one could lift them. However I still treasure a chest in which I now keep blankets and linen: it must be made of the heaviest and hardest wood obtainable. At one time Father brought home a live bandicoot from somewhere, and it ran up and down the passage all night, and then it got lost. I strongly suspect Mother of helping it.

My husband died in 1956 and I had a struggle to educate two girls, Karin fourteen, and Tyra ten. At that time I thought they were too young to be left if I worked full time so it was the Widows Pension, plus Education Department help, Canteens Trust Fund help and State Savings Bank bursaries. In time I gradually did work at home, then part time jobs — at one time I had three jobs going in the week. When I was nearly sixty I was desperate as a job I relied upon folded up, then I saw an advertisement for a stenographer in the Public

Service at Armadale — 100 w.p.m. shorthand. I replied and was taken on — I was six weeks under sixty — and I was there with State Rivers until sixty-five. Early in my time there I sat for 120 w.p.m. exam and passed — that meant an extra 15s per week. Then I had a part time job with West Moorabool Water Board and that lasted until I was about seventy-three.

I often wonder whether my life has been worth anything at all; but when I think of my two daughters and how well they have done, in their careers and through their marriages, I think it must have been.

Hazel Lewis b.1908

THE first thing I remember in life was bawling my eyes out. Mama had bought a painting in a secondhand shop and put it in my old gondola pram to wheel it home. I was hanging on to her long skirt and crying.

'If I buy you a banana will you stop crying?'

I stopped immediately. That painting hung on our wall for many years: a girl clinging to a cross, she had long blonde hair and was draped in cream material with a blue swathe across it. It was huge.

When I was six years old I put on a pretty blue dress and ran across the road to play with a girl. I said, 'Look, I have a new dress.'

She said scornfully, 'It is not a new dress, it is secondhand, all your clothes are secondhand.'

I went home broken-hearted to tell Mum what she said.

'Yes, it is secondhand, but it is paid for. There are no debt collectors knocking on my door,' she replied.

We moved into a house that had a large back yard and were given an old horse named Roany. There were six girls, Gladys, Hilda, Annie, Muriel, Alma, myself (Hazel) and my brother Tommy home at the time. A sister, Margaret, and brother, Jock, were married, and one girl, Millie, was in service. Gladys and Hilda had got certificates to go to work at twelve because of hardship.

The bigger girls would get on Roany, then Tommy would give it a slap and off it would walk. One day the girls were enjoying a ride when Tommy picked up a piece of wood and gave the horse a whack. Roany leapt in the air and tore up the sideway, where it got stuck. My sisters screamed and Mum came running.

'Drag your legs clear and slide down over his rump,' she ordered. It was a wonder that they didn't break their legs.

Tommy got a good talking-to and the next day Mum had the horse taken away. Tommy started to sing:

> Poor old Roany's dead,
> He died for want of breath,
> They put him in a coffin,
> He fell through the bottom,
> Poor old Roany's dead.

When we all started to cry, Tom was warned again not to tease us.

Two days later we were washing our hands in a tin dish on the back verandah, when Tom said, 'I bet that is Roany you are washing your hands with, he was given to the knackery and was boiled down for soap.'

Annie went deathly white and Muriel promptly threw up. I didn't quite understand what he meant, but ran to get Mum. She took one look at Annie and pushed her head down between her knees, then turned and gave Tom a resounding slap right across the face. The mark stayed there for hours.

Mum suspected that Tom had been wagging school, so on Monday morning he was hauled out of bed at six o'clock, given a cut lunch and told not to come home until he had a job. He started work in a butcher's shop and we weren't teased any more.

War broke out in 1914 and my eldest brother Jock enlisted. Two years later Tom put his age up and enlisted too. He was just seventeen when a bomb exploded near him and buried him. They got him out just in time. He was shipped home with impaired hearing. After a time they tried to send him back, but he ran away. He would come home to see Mum who would cook him a meal and put him to bed. If we saw the military police coming down our street we would run in and tell Tom and he would jump over the back fence. Dad thought he was shell-shocked and not fit to go back. He got tired of running and eventually went back and got an honourable discharge.

I was ten when we heard a boy calling out, 'Extra! Extra!' outside the school. The teacher gave me a penny to get her a paper. It said the war was over, and she stood there with tears running down her cheeks, asking us to sing, 'God save the king.'

We lived in North Fitzroy just out of Melbourne city. We used to play rounders and statues under the gas lights. I remember a man coming around on a bike, with a long pole to light the lamps. On a hot night Mum and Dad would sit on the gas box on the front verandah to watch us play. There was no fear of molesters, then, and we could go to someone else's place a few streets away to play, too. Opposite our place was a picture palace and sometimes we would lie on our stomachs on the footpath for a free look under the side door. Or sometimes Mum would say, 'Come on, we will go for a blow on the tram.'

We would sit on the front seat of the dummy on the cable tram where we would get a lovely breeze. The tram was run by an underground cable and a gripman drove it. If we were lucky we would strike the singing gripman with the beautiful tenor voice and he would sing all the way to the terminus and back. After a while Mum would pluck up courage and ask him to sing one of her favourite Italian songs.

The highlight of the year would be the Sunday school picnic when we went right up to South Morang in a drag with two horses. You had to wear your best dress and take a pannikin for your cup of tea. We had lollies and soft drinks and were given balloons; we ran in races for a bag of sweets, then sang all the way home.

Every Saturday we would round up all the kids and have a concert in the Edinburgh Gardens. Some would sing, some would dance, me, I could only turn handsprings but not very well. One day I watched a girl turn handsprings and said, 'I wish I could do them like you'.

She said, 'I will teach you. Keep your legs and back straight and hold your head up for balance.'

I practised all that day and every day, back and legs straight, try and touch the sky with your toes, round and round, over and over. I surprised my friends at the next concert, by tucking my dress into my bloomers and putting on a very good show.

One of my girlfriends was going to learn the piano. I asked Mum could I learn too.

'How much a lesson?' asked Mum.

'One shilling.'

'A shilling?' Mum exclaimed, 'How on earth do you think I could spare a whole shilling, just for a piano lesson?'

Then Miss Alison was going to open a dancing school in Scotsmere Street. I rushed home saying, 'Mum! Mum! Janet is going to learn dancing, can I learn too, only sixpence a week?'

Mum said, 'I'll tell you what I will do. I will make sure you have threepence every Saturday and you can go to the pictures or spend it as you like. That is the best I can do.'

Janet was hopeless at dancing so she left. Then we heard that the Thistle Callisthenic Club was starting in St Luke's Church hall in St Georges Road. Miss Pettingal was going to teach club-swinging, free arm and rods, also little plays with singing. It was only threepence a week, so we were right.

We never missed a Saturday, and when we were put in a concert, no prima donna could have been prouder. Who could forget, 'My Sweet Little Alice Blue Gown', dressed in cheesecloth dyed blue because it was the cheapest material available. It nearly brought the house down. Mum said, 'I was so happy that I cried.'

I said, 'You don't cry when you are happy.' I found out since that you can.

I had just turned twelve when our teacher told us that a Domestic Arts school was opening at Bell Street and wanted

pupils. I begged Mum to let me go, as Janet was going. We would only have two days schooling, one day cooking, one day laundry, half day sewing and half day housewifery.

Mum said, 'What about your schooling?'

I declared that I hated school and would rather learn to cook. She relented and let me go. I loved cooking and was soon cooking for the head teacher's table. When I had a sponge cake put in an exhibition I was ecstatic. Then after eighteen months Mum took ill and asked me to stay home to help her in the house. When she recovered I got a job in a factory, and school days were over.

Every month Mum went to the Young Street Mission to buy clothes for us. I remember her bringing them out after tea and my sisters picking them over.

Mum pulled Annie aside and said, 'I kept this for you. I

heard you say that you would love a costume. It is beautiful material.'

It was grey and too big, so Annie sat down and unpicked every stitch very carefully, turned it inside out and made it up again to fit her. She was just fourteen.

Mum didn't have any money to spare the next month, but she went just the same as she enjoyed the company and they sang hymns, then had a cup of tea and biscuits. When everything was nearly sold the sister in charge gathered everything up that was left and said to Mum, 'You can have it for a penny.'

Mum rolled it into a bundle and brought it home. When we unrolled it after tea, there were bloomers, petticoats, two washed-out dresses, socks, two men's coats and a dainty blouse which had pearls instead of buttons, which Annie made a grab for. In her costume and pretty blouse she looked like a million pounds. She wore that outfit until she was married.

I was fifteen and a half before I was allowed to go to a dance with my sister. Muriel said, 'Never dance with a boy that brings pumps to change into, they are always corks (rotten dancers).' Muriel was tall and fair and beautiful and won lots of competitions. Every lunchtime at work we bolted down our sandwiches and danced to the girls singing the latest hits.

Muriel said, 'Don't sit with those kids at the dance, good dancers won't look at you, better to stand alone.'

The next dance we went to, Muriel said, 'Come and say hello to me just as the music starts.' She was always booked dances ahead.

When a chap asked her to dance she said, 'I am sorry, I am booked for the next two, but will save the third for you.' She turned to smile at me, so the chap asked me to dance. It was the best that I had ever danced.

From then on I was in. How conceited I became. I took a leaf out of Muriel's book — if a cork asked her to dance she would disdainfully say, 'No'. And after all that, she married a chap who didn't like dancing. But the Depression came, they both lost their jobs and had to come home to live.

Tommy was always out of work, so I took my pay packet home unopened; we had to eat. With winter drawing near, Mum bought all the suits and overcoats and thick jumpers that nobody wanted, unpicked them and the linings, washed them, then cut them into squares and made them into patchwork quilts. She lined the backs with winceyette; they were as good as three blankets.

We had a good hot meal every night. Mostly tripe or stews or sausages with home-grown vegetables and two potatoes to fill us up. Mum put one slice of bread on every plate; if we wanted another she would say, 'Butter or jam, not both.' Breakfast was always porridge and golden syrup till later when things got better, then she cooked us bacon and eggs.

The war must have done something to Tommy. He could not hold a job and he and Dad started to argue. Dad was getting old but had to keep working, carrying a hod filled with bricks. There were eight of us at home, but only Dad, Gladys and I were working. I don't know how Mum kept food on the table. Tommy would not lower his dignity to queue for sustenance, or 'susso' as everyone called it, but he always had cigarettes to smoke.

I remember Tom cutting cardboard to fit inside his shoes when the soles were wearing out. He scorned the coats and jumpers that Mum brought home, but when it got really cold he was glad of them. What false pride he had. When he tried to cadge threepence off me for cigarettes I told him straight, 'I don't have threepence, all my wages go into the house so that we can eat.'

It was only the love of a good mother that kept the family together and made the struggle worthwhile.

When we had been married for three and a half years, George won a baby's chair in a raffle and said to me, 'Now fill it!' Next month I told him I was pregnant, and we were thrilled to bits. I was very well and had a baby boy; we named him George Laurence, but called him Laurie.

I used to visit mum every week and would wheel the pram proudly through the streets, looking in shop windows on the way. Beckwith's the butcher had 5 lbs of forequarter chops on for 1s. What a bargain. They were usually 5d per pound.

When I got home I picked them over; there were two leg chops among them, so I grilled them for tea. Next night I put four chops in the baking dish, covered them with onions, then thick slices of potato, added a little water and baked them (haricot chops). Next day I put all the chops on to boil, made barley broth out of the gravy, took four chops out and curried them, serving them on a bed of rice. On Friday I cut all the meat off the rest of the chops and made a fricassée with carrots, onion and peas. We ate like lords all the week for only one shilling. I kept all the fat off the chops and, with what Georgie's mum saved for me, made my own soap.

We bought an old bomb of a car for £15. It was a tourer but had no side curtains. George's parents had taken a country hotel at Riddell, about twenty-five miles from Melbourne and invited us up for weekends. His father did not enjoy good health, so George worked in the bar all Saturday afternoon for him. We would leave the back seat of the car home, so that we could bring home a load of wood. Every Sunday morning my sister-in-law Edna, and I would walk along the railway line to pick up lumps of coal. We always ended up with a bucket full.

What with the wood and coal, growing our own vegetables, making our own soap, and George being allowed a quarter loaf of bread a day, we lived very cheaply and I could save more than half his wages.

We were offered a little run-down hotel at Bulla, fifteen miles from Melbourne when Laurie was eleven months, for £2 10s a week and stay as long as we liked. It was on the main road, only nine miles from Essendon.

When we asked George's mum what she thought, she said, 'You are a good cook and George is well-liked in the bar, so you can't go wrong.'

A week before we took the hotel George had misgivings. He said, 'I am giving up a steady job and £4 6s a week.'

I said, 'I have every confidence in you, we are young and strong, look ahead not back, we'll be all right.' And we were.

The hotel at Bulla was shabby and dirty. We bought new lino for the parlours and I paid 2s 6d a yard for congoleum for the dining room. (It was still down twenty-five years later!) That was 1934.

I had to get used to a wood stove; my hands were ruined but everything cooked beautifully. Lovely apple pies, their tops golden brown, and the scones rose high and light. You can't beat a roast from the wood stove and plum puddings simmering on the side of the stove for six hours kept a long time. I soon got known for putting on a good meal, three courses for 1s 6d.

Then I had a little girl. I called her Joan. She was like a princess with her long fair hair and hazel eyes.

It was not long before we discarded the old furniture and bought new, but kept our own suite. We made some good friends; it was more like a club than a pub. The men brought their wives every Saturday afternoon, and when they were going they used to say, 'See you in church.' Customers not in the know would say, 'Isn't it lovely that you all meet in church?'

What they didn't know was that we had a service every Sunday night from five o'clock until six-thirty, right in our parlour for a drink. Georgie used to say the cops would be home for their tea then, and we would be safe. This went on for years and we were never caught.

Then I became pregnant again. I said, 'How many children are we going to have?'

'Oh,' Georgie said, 'we can afford this one, so let your head go.'

With the other two I had had to shop at Coles. I bought lovely nighties and dressing gown and slippers to match. Rodney kept me in labour for thirty-six hours, but he was a perfect baby.

The business continued to prosper and we started to cater for the Hunt Club and cooked for fifty to sixty people. We were invited to a ball and I bought my first evening dress for a long while. We vowed to go more often.

Less than two years later I said to George, 'You have done it again.'

'Done what?' he asked innocently.

'Made me pregnant.'

'Oh no, not again.'

'You will have to do something after this,' I stated, but of course he never did. When I was five months pregnant, the greatest sorrow of my life occurred. I lost my mum. She was seventy-one. I cried for months, then had to pull myself together for the sake of the baby.

We had another son, Geoffrey. He was a thin little baby, but seemed contented. He was a great talker, and at fifteen months you could have a sensible conversation with him. When he was sixteen months old his little sister was born, Pamela Joy. She was a redhead and George called her his strawberry blonde; she was plump and cuddly and Geoff and she got on well together.

Then I really did put my foot down, and said, 'No more children.' I had two babies and three other children under eight years. It was no fun to knock off an enormous wash to go to hospital to have a baby. I said, 'We are lucky, they are all healthy and strong and besides, I am thirty-three and have done my duty.'

Sometimes we had help and sometimes not. I'll never forget having a very fat woman working for us, she couldn't get on her knees to polish the floors so stood up to do it. Rodney couldn't resist the target and stuck a fork in her backside. She left the next day.

Then we had Mack, she was a good worker and told us she didn't drink. That suited us fine, so when it came to New Year's Eve I asked her would she like a lemonade as it was so hot. She replied that she would have a whisky.

'That is a very strong drink.'

'Don't worry,' she said, 'I am used to it. I haven't had a drink for a fortnight but feel like one tonight.'

Boy, did she get full, and when we locked up at two in the morning she said, 'Give me a bottle of beer and I will be right in the morning.'

We did that, and an hour later she was back wanting another one. 'Be fair,' I told her, 'you know we have a crowd booked in for dinner tomorrow.'

'Just one more,' she said.

George exploded, and pushed her out of the room telling her where she could go. She swore at him, calling him some names that I had never heard before in my life. He told her to pack her bags and go. She did that, and I was on my own again.

Then came Daphne. She wasn't a bad worker but a shocking cook. George asked me, 'Can't you cook *my* meals?'

'No, not with a new baby to look after and all the washing to do.'

When it was Daphne's day off I was pleased, as I was sick of her cooking, too. George drove her to the nearest tram, and when he got back he said, 'Please, Love, a nice steak, and vegies not all mashed up, and one of your lovely sweets.'

After I put the baby down to sleep I thought I would make a big pot of soup first. I opened the cupboard and there was not a pot to be seen. I looked everywhere, even in her room, nothing!

I asked George, 'Did Daphne take a case with her?'

'No, only a handbag.'

I said, 'Well that's funny, I can't find a thing to cook in.'

'Don't tell me she has thrown everything out.'

'Well, seeing I can't cook, I may as well boil up the nappies,' I said.

I went to the wash-house which was across the yard, and found a copper full of water. I dived the dipper in, when clunk, it hit something pretty hard. I put my hands in, and out came all the pots and pans and baking dishes. It was a very large copper — she couldn't have washed up anything for days. I called George; he couldn't believe his eyes.

He said, 'Give them to me, I will polish them up.'

After the washing I cooked us a nice meal. George said, 'Cook enough for a week.'

'She would only burn it if I did.'

The next week Daphne asked for a few days off to see her daughter, and took her case. We never saw her again.

Then came Mrs X. I cooked her a three-course meal, and she went straight to bed. Next morning there was no sign of her; I went to her room, the bed hadn't been slept in. I rang the Agency and asked, 'Have you any more lunatics down there that want a free meal?'

Then there was Mrs B. Anything she didn't want to do she would say, 'I can't do that.'

She couldn't iron silk, so I had to iron nearly all the children's clothes, even though they were only artificial silk. The crunch came when George came out and saw me blacking the stove, because she couldn't do that. He told her to pull her weight or get out. She went.

Then later we had Mrs D., but everyone called her 'Lovey'. She could iron beautifully, but she couldn't wash. After two weeks I told George, 'My washing has a distinct grey tinge, I can't stand that.'

'Yes,' he answered, 'and my socks are hard, they make my feet ache. I am too much on my feet to put up with that. You will just have to put them aside and wash them yourself.'

I went out to wash with her, and could see what she was doing wrong. I told her I liked my washing rinsed twice, then blued. I washed the socks myself.

'Has there been a complaint about the socks?' she asked.

'Yes.'

'You know, I used to work for the Lord Mayor of Melbourne, and "Lovey", he said to me, "you cook and iron like a dream, but you can't wash socks".'

'Yes, Lovey,' I replied, 'the dirt is on the outside, but the perspiration is on the inside, so they must be washed both sides.'

'Well,' she exclaimed, 'you are only half my age, but you have taught me something.'

142

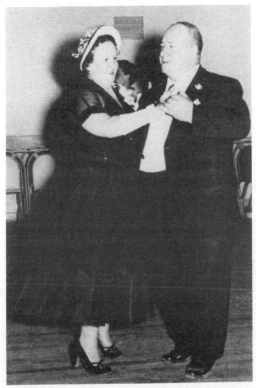
Hazel and George

Very early in our marriage I learned that if George said, 'We must do this, or paint that,' it meant me. He hardly knew which end of a paint brush to use. Only once did he ever use one, which was when we bought our £15 car.

He said, 'It looks awful, we must paint it.'

'No. You paint it. I have a young baby and am making soap, jam and pickles, you paint it.'

He bought the paint brush and started. He painted half of it. I finished it and painted the mudguards black. It didn't look too bad.

When I said that the upstairs of the hotel wanted painting he got a quote. It was very high, so he said, 'We will get the walls and ceiling done, but the main cost is in painting all those old-fashioned doors. We will have to do them ourselves.'

143

I said, 'I will do them. But don't call me downstairs for every little thing. I can't put the brush down and clean my hands all the time.'

He agreed but still allowed friends to come up. It was very hot with the blinds sky high and all the windows and doors open.

I said to George, 'If I knock on the floor three times with the heel of my shoe, it means I want a beer.'

He grinned, 'And if I knock twice on the counter it means you're not getting one.'

One hot day he brought me a pot without me knocking. I said, aghast, 'Only men drink pots.'

'You are working like a man. Enjoy it, Love,' he replied.

There were nine of those old-fashioned doors, with four panels in each door and I had to get paint into all those little grooves, then I painted the foot high skirting boards.

The one thing I can't accept in my life was that I was born in the age when children had to be seen but not heard. We were told never to speak unless spoken to. When I started to mix with others than my family I could not start a conversation. In company I would be a good listener. If I did venture an opinion someone would only have to argue and I would clam up, even though I knew I was right. If I had a difference of opinion with my husband, he would only have to shout at me to bring tears to my eyes.

How I envied others who would walk into a room and take complete charge of it, as much as to say, 'Here I am, look at me.' It was a terrible ordeal for me to have to go into the bar to serve a couple of men and try to make conversation. The busier it was the better I liked it for I wouldn't have time to talk to anyone. I don't think I could have changed it, it was just the time I was born in . . . I could have made much more of myself if only I was encouraged to have confidence.

144

Florence

Florence Clover b.1908

UNTIL I had seen the article about 'Write about your life' in the *Weekly Times* I had never even thought about writing anything, much less about my life. Although I was happy with life it never struck me as being interesting to anybody else. But just recently, one of our little grandsons told his pre-school teacher, 'My gran makes up stories out of her mouth, she does.' My own children have often said, 'Mum, why don't you write down the stories that you tell us?' and recently my eldest daughter reminded me again.

'Do you remember the pretty little cup you had, Mum, with a little house painted on it, and when any of us were sick in bed you would bring in the cup with soup or jelly and while we were eating you would tell us about little Margarita who supposedly lived in the little house on the cup and every time you told us a different adventure?'

It dated from my fifth birthday and my parents' silver wedding anniversary. I was the tenth of twelve children. Nothing as beautiful had ever come my way before this pink fluted cup and saucer.

Dad was a carpenter and to move his timber and tools to various jobs he used a hand truck he'd made himself. It had two large wheels and after pushing it a couple of miles, he must have been very tired. Dad and Mum were both English born and migrated here in 1888. Mum's family were very well-to-do and she often told us about the servants they had and different tutors. She also learnt French, music and painting. At the tea table only French was allowed to be spoken when they had a French governess.

As I got older I often wondered how she coped, with babies arriving in quick succession and not much money, no help in the house and Dad always liking his meals right on the dot as well. All of the babies were born at home, with the assistance of a midwife, and a doctor — if he got there on time. My mother was forty years old when I was born, the tenth girl, and two boys came after me.

Dad loved and was proud of us but I can't see him attending to a baby in any way. He was a reserved straight-backed Englishman and very strict. We all had to attend Church and Sunday school; we had our own pew which filled and overflowed. We always had a 10 o'clock curfew if any of us girls went out in the evening.

Mum must have decided to be an Australian as soon as she landed here. She was so friendly and she would quickly get into conversations on train or tram journeys. They lived first at Richmond then St Kilda. I went to St Kilda Park state school.

Sometimes on a rainy day Mum would turn up at the school with a cut lunch for us. We usually went home. She must have been soaked when she got there but I don't remember being grateful as Mum carried our lunch in a basket and no other children had their lunch in a basket nor had they sandwiches like ours, called 'matrimony', two slices of bread and margarine with stale cake in between. Margarine wasn't the sophisticated product then that it is now. One slice of bread with butter was our treat on Sunday nights. There was always plenty of golden syrup or treacle, though. But bread and dripping with tomato was favourite. My mouth waters today when I just think of it because Mum would pack those sandwiches and off we would all go picnicking to spend the whole day at the beach if it was hot. A lovely stretch of an unspoiled St Kilda beach we often had just to ourselves, or we would walk right down to the bluff at

Point Ormond, or even just to the Blessington Street Gardens if the day was cool. But here there were swings and see-saws. You jumped off the swing when you reached the highest point, sailing through the air to land on your feet. To get a ride on the merry-go-round we would have to collect a bundle of rags to give to the man to polish all the brass. In return we were given one ticket. So we took it in turns to collect the rags.

My eldest sister Nell was clever with needle and thread and always unpicked the clothing sent from elderly relations in England: good material magically re-made into well fitting school and play clothes for us younger ones. Mum knitted woollen singlets and socks for us on a knitting machine. I don't know where it came from. It was nothing like those today but it did the job very well. On Saturday mornings we would get up at 6.30 a.m. and Mum would take a couple of us with her to Victoria Market. We sat on the front of the 'dummy' on the tram and loved following Mum round all the stalls till the baskets were full of vegetables and fruit.

Christmas was always so special. Dad's large workshop was cleared, all the timber stacked to one side with a lot of space left in the middle. On Christmas Eve our stockings were hung on a string along the benches, from the youngest's up to Dad's, and nobody was allowed in till after breakfast and the dishes were done. Then we would all troop in and stockings emptied strictly to order, beginning with the youngest. Then it was time for church. Mum and a couple of older ones stayed behind to get the dinner.

After dinner the dishes were done and then the fun would start. We might be joined by boyfriends of the older girls. We would have peanut and potato races, games we made up and everyone played and scored points. 'Uncle Toby', a large wooden face on a hinge could be knocked over with soft balls; sides were picked. Mrs Gibbons, a very very tall lady, always visited us and handed out sweets. It was years before I discovered that it was one sister sitting on the shoulders of another, although I often wondered why she always wore the same long cloak and funny hat. Then there was the Shadow Pantomime, performed behind a sheet lit up by a bright light. The biggest thrill was to be chosen to take part. After Boxing Day everything was put back to wait for another year.

I went to Melbourne High School and eventually became a junior teacher at South Melbourne primary school. Attending classes for teacher-training after school I passed yearly exams until I was entitled to apply for a 'one teacher country school'. I went to the Mallee in 1927. Erected by the people of the district the building was quite old, unlined, with a bare wooden floor. It did have a ceiling, but none of it had ever seen a touch of paint. But we gathered pictures, pasted them on cardboard and brightened the room with a couple of vases of gum tips.

Its one saving grace was a big fireplace and the whole school, twelve pupils ranging from grades 1 to 8, would sometimes spend an hour or so picking up firewood from under the box trees at the back of the school. Occasionally we would get a few mallee roots brought which would make beautiful fires. On frosty mornings I would light the fire as soon as I arrived and with the door closed a cosy schoolroom would soon be ready for the children. Some had a few miles to travel, a few came on horseback, one family in a gig, and others walked.

On my first day, which I spent mostly getting to know my pupils, there was a girl of thirteen who seemed rather plumper than the others, though not especially so. She attended for two days and was absent the rest of the week and you can imagine my consternation and also of the whole district, when she was rushed to the hospital and gave birth to a baby. I never saw her again as she was taken away immediately and the whole affair was hushed up. She lived with an aunt who apparently had not noticed anything amiss.

Until I went to live in the Mallee I had no idea of the uses to be had from kerosene tins and cases. The cases, stacked in different ways, were used for shelves, kitchen dressers; dressing tables — with a coat of paint and a cretonne curtain down the front looked quite attractive. If a number of visitors came and there were not enough chairs to go round, a couple of cases turned on their ends served theirs. Tops cut out of the tins with the edges rolled over meant water for baths could be heated on the stove, and these were used to boil the clothes in on washing day. Cut in half diagonally and bent outwards forming two triangular troughs with a light wooden frame to hold them provided a washing-up dish and drainer. Few houses had sinks with water laid on. It was carried in from an outside tank in a kerosene tin. Ironing was not an enviable job in summer as the stove had to be well stoked up to heat the flat irons, or the Mrs Potts irons which had a detachable wooden handle.

Trips into town 12 miles away were rare, but sometimes the younger ones would go in to a picture show in an old ute. Teacher was lucky, always offered the front seat with floorboards to rest her feet on, but the others dangled their legs over the side. We'd pick up a couple of neighbours on the way, and then sing all the road home. About every three months a dance would be held in the school. Candles were scraped and rubbed into the floor but it was never 'fast'. In fact, it was rather rough, but nobody seemed to mind. Some families would bring lanterns, others the copper and a huge teapot. The boiling of the copper, the tea-making and serving was always done by the men. Cecil Clover whom I later married made the music with a button accordion. He still plays this and the grandchildren love it.

Early in our marriage Cecil and I owned a small truck boasting a home-made cabin and tray on it. Most of our income came from carting wheat, in bags, which had to be hand loaded, unloaded and stacked. But 1934, when our first baby was twelve months old, was a drought year, with no wheat carting or any other. Then we heard from an uncle in the centre of New South Wales the good news that there was 'plenty of wheat up that way'.

At Ungarie, when we got there, the wheat wasn't quite ready so Cecil pitched hay in the paddock for 7s 6d a day. This meant pitching the sheaves, no bales then, on to the

The small truck with home-made cabin and tray loaded with mallee roots

truck and then off the truck on to the hay stack. It wasn't an eight-hour day, either! But it was work, and after the wheat carting was finished all round the district, we were able to go home with £100. What riches they were! The money started off our savings and not long after we were able to pay a deposit on a bigger, brand new truck, which led to more work and in a couple of years to building our own home. By then we had three children and all this time had been sharing a house with Cecil's parents.

As well as wheat and general carting we went in for poultry farming — incubators, brooders, the lot. Also, having a large paddock at the back we bought a few cows and built up a milk round. We hired a man to help with the milking but the delivering, night and morning, had to be done seven days a week. The three older children, Sue, Del and Joe, helped deliver, before and after school. There were cans and billies as well as milking machines to scour, left-over milk to be separated, cream and eggs to be served to customers at all hours, as well as generally looking after the poultry, cleaning and packing the eggs. The children helped with everything. By this time we were the happy parents of two more girls Noelene and Rikki.

We kept this up for a few years, finding it increasingly difficult. And it didn't seem fair to the children. If we did make time to take them anywhere we always had to leave early to milk and deliver. We figured that if we moved south to a dairying property, amongst dairy farmers, milk would be picked up at the gate, and sporting and social fixtures would be timed to suit the dairy farmers. And it was so.

When we moved to Timboon in 1953, we found people so friendly. The majority of them seemed to have cleared their blocks the hard way, with an axe, or were still doing so.

On the day of our removal the truck with our furniture broke down and we didn't reach our little farm till ten o'clock at night. It was pouring with rain. The people from whom we had bought the farm had not yet moved out which was a blessing in disguise. Electricity had not yet come along that road. Neighbours from nearby were soon on the scene to help and took Sue and Del over to their place to sleep. We were thankful just to put our mattresses and blankets on the floor — and sleep!

But that farm was too small. We found another out of town, but it was not cleared and had only a tiny tumbledown house on it. There were only wallaby tracks through the thick undergrowth. But we took it on — still living and milking on the small one. In between milkings, Cecil and Joe and often myself would travel up to the other to get some of it cleared.

We hired a bulldozer and driver to push down the larger trees but couldn't afford to have it pushed into windrows — long heaps parallel to each other across the paddocks. But we had a horse and sled to help cart the logs into heaps and swing and chain saws to cut the suitable ones into firewood, which we sold. The home-made sled consisted of two long logs for runners with a platform built over them. This sounds like hard work, but when we talked with people who had been in the district for twenty years or more their experiences made our task seem easy. One family had lived in a tent for some years and cleared a lot of their block with an axe and a horse and sled and when they had finally come to a few cows, milked them by hand. The first calf this man bought was carried home on his shoulders.

Another old timer told us how in his young days he would

start milking, by hand, at 3 a.m., then separate and take the cream to the factory by horse and cart. By the time the calves were fed and skim milk taken to the pigs and all the cleaning up done, it was time to start the afternoon milking. How much lighter our own task seemed then!

After the big logs had been taken out, came the 'emu bobbing'. This is where I came in handy as it means picking up the smaller branches, roots, etc., piling them into heaps and burning them. Then came ploughing, then more emu bobbing until it was clear enough to fence and sow to pasture.

While the pastures were becoming established we turned our minds to building a new house. The little one was beyond repair. Cecil and Joe, with the help of a builder at weekends were to build it themselves. I drew up the plans.

Many changes have taken place since that time. Our place is cleared, and the one next door, and the one over the road. Shelter belts of natural bush have been left and we have planted many wind breaks of native trees. Electricity is here and milk tankers come right up to the dairy and collect the milk from refrigerated vats. All of our children have married and Joe and his wife Jean built their home near ours. They run the farm and Cecil and I sit back and pursue our hobbies.

When we learned that Cecil's lung cancer had been arrested the doctor agreed that we might spend our annual holiday visiting our daughter in Brisbane. Plenty of advice forthcoming — 'Why don't you fly up?' or, 'Go by train, and put the car on, too.' It would take much more than advice to get Cecil in an aeroplane.

The car trip was uncomplicated. We didn't hurry, stayed at motels, and really enjoyed the trip. Brisbane is always a happy place for us. Our three grand-daughters are delightful, we all get along well together. When Jannine, fifteen, said to me, 'Gran, I'm going to take you out for a day in the city, if you'd like to come,' I was thrilled. 'We will look around the shops and go to a movie, if there is one you'd like to see, but I've got to ask Dad first to see if I can have a day off school.'

Permission granted, and off we went in the early morning catching the school train. A number of her school mates were introduced to me. They included me in their chatter — which seemed very similar to the topics we used to talk about years ago, except for a few new expressions that cropped up.

We went to the Town Hall first and took the two lifts right up to the clock tower, then we did a bit of looking and shopping, walked around a fun parlour, had lunch and decided to see 'Tess'. We both enjoyed it, but for me it was a lovely, lovely day. Just to have been asked.

School holidays are nice. We see more of our family and grandchildren. Our son and daughter-in-law live only about 2 chain — sorry, 43 metres — away from us. Our youngest daughter and three children come up by train. They all love the farm life. It is always five children here or five children there, or none at either place, which means there are five children at the haystack or down the paddock somewhere.

Time spent with children, even grown-up children, is never wasted.

Elsie

Elsie Burns b.1908

I was born in Steiglitz, Victoria, an old goldmining town. My parents moved to Daylesford a year later but in 1915 we moved back to Steiglitz to my grandmother's farm where my father lived as a boy.

There was plenty of work to be done on the farm; oats and barley crops to be sown, potato crop to be planted and kept hoed and vegetables to be grown and weeded, an orchard of fruit trees to be pruned: apple trees, peaches, pears, plums, cherries, quinces. There was a huge mulberry tree, and hedges of gooseberries and black and red currants, raspberries and blackberries, and one grape vine. Around the house was a flower garden of half an acre, with rose trees of every colour and variety. Three large pepper trees and two laburnums shaded the house; a beautiful big lilac and sweet-smelling woodbine grew at the front, marvellous perfume on a frosty morning.

There were lavenders and daphnes, rosemary; bulbs coming up everywhere — daffodils, jonquils, pokers, iris, snowdrops and lily-of-the-valley. In summer came Christmas lily, pink and red and white madonna, white and blue agapanthus; nerines and freesias everywhere. My favourites were the aquilegias which Grandmother called 'granny's bonnets' that grew among a profusion of pansies, violets, daisies, nasturtiums, marigolds, love-in-the-mist, chrysanthemums and carnations. Almost every flower there was, my grandmother had in her garden.

The paths were paved with flat water-worn stones brought up from the creek bed. Where the creek turned at the front gate and below the waterfall there were large water holes. Their water kept the garden and vegetables lush in summertime. Water was also stored in dams which filled from hillsides when the rains came. The overflow drain from the dam grew watercress, mint, thyme, marjoram, garlic and aniseed. Grandmother made nettle tea and used dandelion and dock root for medicine. She also used a wild mint which grew in the creek.

The creek ran from miles up beyond our farm in a half circle and then turned and flowed past the township where it joined another creek then on to another river before it reached the sea. We fished in the river for blackfish and eels and the sweet redfin from the reservoirs; we learned to swim in the waterholes in summer and in winter we tobogganed down the hillsides. In summer when the grass was long and dry we slid down on flat pieces of tin turned up in front to tuck our toes in — they were very fast. We rolled rocks down the steep hills into the gullies below, looked for birds' nests in the trees and found beehives in their hollows. My eldest brother gathered swarms of bees which settled in the orchard, until he had thirty boxes of hives. He used to extract the honey and my mother would bottle it.

We kept cows, goats and sheep on the farm and once had a pig when we made our own bacon. Mother taught me how to make bread and cakes, and jam and preserves when the fruit was ready. At school we were taught First Aid which was just as well as my brother was able to treat his own snake bite which saved his life. He had to walk five miles home before he could get medical treatment.

At thirteen I sat for my Merit certificate, passed well and the teacher tried to convince my parents I should go on to high school and become a teacher. I would have liked that; I loved learning, and teaching others, but Mother needed me at home. Since her recent last baby she had thrombosis in her leg and needed to rest it. When the school holidays were

155

over and the rest of the family went off to school I cried. But then I soon settled down and loved helping, especially taking care of the baby.

There was plenty to be done: getting the breakfast, cutting lunches which I had done for years anyway, and seeing the children were ready and off on time, then the housework. Doing the washing was new to me — I had already been helping with ironing and mending. I found the washing hard work, using a copper on an open fire, carrying buckets of water and lifting into the washtubs. Clothes props were hard to handle when the sheets were wet on the line.

Soon I could make butter in the churn and pat it into pounds. We sold butter to the townspeople, also milk, cream, vegetables and potatoes. I knitted jumpers for the family, socks and even long socks for myself. We needed warm clothing for nine months of the year; the frosts were very severe but only once did we have snow. I liked summer-time and swimming, log fires in winter and gardening in spring.

From my sixteenth birthday I learned to play the violin and practised every spare minute I had. Soon my teacher and I could play together, opera tunes, then Irish jigs and Scottish reels and the waltzes which I liked best of all. Later on, my brother bought two harps, one a zither and the other a mandolin played with a little wooden hammer. He and I both could soon play them. Then came a mandolin and banjo. We became a musical family and our parents taught us how to dance. What did we do before radio and television? We worked, we played, we sang and danced, we communicated and we were a happy family.

With the township folk we formed a social committee to run dances in the courthouse which had been vacant and worked hard waxing the floor for dancing. For supper the committee made sandwiches and we baked lovely sponges and cream cakes and served tea and coffee. Everyone danced, the parents and the young, whole families; quadrilles (first set Lancers, the Alberts, Royal Irish Exines, and Waltz of Cotillions).

We waltzed and had ordinary and progressive barn

dances early in the programme where everyone changed partners until all had danced with everyone then back to their original partners. We had the Highland Schottische, Polka, Galop, Varsoviena which really rocked the wooden floor. Later we learned the Onestep and Foxtrot, the Veleta Waltz and the prettiest dance of all, the Pride of Erin. The only thing we liked about the Charleston was the learning how to do it.

With money made from the dances we built a tennis court, formed a club and played the tennis folk from surrounding districts.

When the Depression came our district dwindled to just a few families. We had no local trade so I had to find work somewhere to bring home some money as we still had to buy flour and sugar, odd groceries and clothes. I found a job in Geelong as mother's help in a family of six at 25s a week, full board and a small room to myself. I sent home £1 each week and kept 5s for fares and clothing.

In the summer I used to rise early to go for a swim. Sunday evenings I went to church and every Thursday night was given a complimentary pass to the pictures. I saw the first talkies, *Sonny Boy* among them. Every Saturday night I went to old-time dances in the East Library Hall; we paid 1s at the door, they began at 8 p.m. sharp and went till 11 p.m.; no supper, I was in bed before midnight. Our country dances always provided supper and we danced until two or three o'clock in the morning. I still went home to the dances whenever I could get a weekend off work.

My mother wrote to me every Sunday, and often the brother who stayed at home to help on the farm and the one working on the Bonang Highway in Gippsland wrote as well. Two sisters came down to Geelong to take jobs like mine. We missed the bush life and whenever we could would take a tram to its terminus and walk the surrounding hills. We pooled our wages and bought clothing for our parents and the two younger ones at home. My wages had been reduced to £1, then 17s 6d then to 15s so we did not have much to spend. It was hard on the ones without any work at all.

Geelong set up a soup kitchen where people could go for a

157

bowl of soup; later they were given a few groceries. Girls from the country would write and beg us to find jobs for them in Geelong. Girls could often get jobs when there were none available for the men. My sisters and I were better off than shop assistants who had to pay their board with their wages. Nurses in training at the hospital were being paid only 6s per week.

Pneumonia put me in hospital for a few weeks. Sister gave me a cough elixir that she said the poor old man in the next ward didn't need, when my cough had become particularly troublesome. One night I said, 'This is very nice medicine.'

'Yes,' she answered, 'yours is finished and he won't need any more of it, he died.'

Though I eventually returned to my job I couldn't properly regain my strength and the doctor suggested I needed to go to a hot dry climate to dry up my lungs, either the Riverina or the Mallee. So I joined a cousin in Corowa who was a dressmaker and needed an assistant to sew hems, put on buttons and press-studs, pin in tucks and pull out tacking threads, make cups of tea and mind the baby. Instead of wages I asked her to teach me the art of cutting out and dressmaking and fitting, which she did.

So gradually I learned to stand on my own, live my own life and find an easier way of earning a living. At least until I married a Mallee farmer at Ouyen, the hottest spot in Victoria, in 1936.

By the time World War II came, I had two small children and another on the way. My husband, as a farmer, was exempted from war service. Our first home, on the main road at Ouyen, was of four rooms with verandahs back and front.

We furnished three rooms — bedroom, lounge-dining and kitchen — for £75 with a bonus of secondhand Singer treadle sewing machine. This bargain consisted of a dining table with six chairs and a buffet with leadlight doors and a large drawer; a three-piece leather covered lounge suite, wooden fireside kerb, two lace curtains, and a 12 foot square of congoleum floor covering and fireside mat; a kitchen suite with 6 foot dresser, large pine table and six chairs, 12 foot square congoleum, and crossover curtains for the window; a bedroom suite of double bed with walnut bed ends, dressing table with full-length mirror, a large ladies wardrobe and gents 'robe, a double mattress, 12 foot square congoleum, lace curtains and two large mats. There was patterned linoleum for the twelve feet long passage way.

Our first move from that home was to the farmhouse where my husband had grown up. His widowed mother and younger brothers and sister left it to live near the township. I did not like the farmhouse, it was too big and hard to keep clean and had no conveniences. The only water supply was one tank of rain water, used for drinking and cooking. All other water for washing and bathing had to be carted from the dam filled by channel once a year. Lights were kerosene lamps. Milk, cream, butter and meat were kept in a Coolgardie safe on the verandah. This was efficient but needed a lot of attention during high temperatures and wind.

The year before World War II the Mallee had one of its

worst droughts. There was no wheat to sell, not enough for next year's seed and the dust storms had to be seen to be believed. The dust smothered everything; sandhills moved or built up in different places. Even in places the railway line was completely covered.

A commercial traveller called in one day during a very bad blow; I was busy with the broom trying to keep the kitchen clear. He greeted me with, 'Put away your broom, lady, your neighbour is using a shovel.' And really, she was. A sandhill had built up behind her back door and as fast as she shovelled it away it still trickled in, like eggtimer salt. I was lucky our house was built high off the ground.

When the temperature reached 116 degrees Fahrenheit in the shade that year most of the fowls died: only the ones sheltering under the house lived. My baby girl was big enough to sit and play in her bath with some water and the toddler son hopped in and out of his bath of water as he wished.

With the truck we often got bogged in the dry sand banked up on the road. Sometimes it was funny, but it wasn't the evening my husband's sister was married. The wedding was to be Christmas Eve and my husband was to be best man, the breakfast at Mother's home. It was a late evening wedding.

I had made cream cakes for the tables. About halfway in, the truck bogged in a new sandhill. Carefully we scraped the sand from the wheels only to bog again every few yards. We were still there at 10 p.m. The wedding and the breakfast would be over by then. We could not believe that no-one had come to look for us. Only afterwards did we realise that with so many tracks through paddocks, any one of which we might have taken, they would hardly have known which way to come so probably hoped for the best, expecting us to turn up at any time.

The baby wasn't keen on a cold bottle and we had only the cream cakes to eat. My husband set off to walk into the township and his brother came out in his utility to pick us up. Twice on the way in, flames flared up from the floor of the ute around my baby's shawl and twice we jumped out. The first time we were travelling slowly but the second time was faster. With my baby in my arms I rolled over and over and then realised why he had yelled, 'Don't jump!' Luckily we were not hurt and were able to put the fire out with sand. Baby screamed all the way in; she was not hurt, only frightened.

The 1939 crop was a bumper one to make up for the drought the year before. The only help my husband had to take off the harvest was one brother and the hired help of an elderly man and his young son. They used a tractor and header and horses and harvester which were slower. Each day a fresh team of horses was harnessed and taken out to relieve the first team soon after midday. A younger brother just left school was given this job.

He brought the first team of horses back from the paddock, unharnessed, watered and fed them. He was a very happy lad and good company. He took lunches out to the men, milked the cow, fed the calf and pigs and fowls, then brought wood for me to the kitchen. I had only a wood stove with an iron fountain and kettle for the hot water.

We found it a great hardship when food was rationed, tea especially because the men needed it so much when working out in the paddocks in the heat and dust. Cocoa and coffee were not as good. When we could not get these we made a substitute coffee by roasting wheat and treacle in the oven. With boiling water it made a drink unlike either tea or coffee but was better than just water. As well as tea rationing, sugar, clothing and petrol were rationed. Coupons as well as money were needed. When the Government issued identity cards there were ration books for each person allowing a limited amount of tea, sugar and clothing.

Because I made our clothes I had clothing coupons to swap for tea coupons. A whole book of clothing coupons was needed for one overcoat for a man. We were lucky to be in a warm climate. Petrol coupons had to be claimed for vehicles. Many groceries were unobtainable or in short supply. I usually bought jam by 6 lb tins. During harvest I rang the grocer to send a tin of jam by the mailman who brought our bread also.

I had to drive with horse and cart to the mailbox on the road two miles away, taking the children with me. There was a small 1½ lb tin of jam with the bread. The men came in for lunch, ate all of it for lunch with cream on their fresh bread. I didn't even get a lick of the spoon.

In January 1942 my father died and I couldn't even go to his funeral. Railway services had been drastically cut so trains were infrequent and all our petrol ration had to be used for carting in the wheat harvest. I now had four children, two boys and two girls. I was very happy with them, but very tired too. As well as my own family I had to cook and wash for those of my husband's family who lived with us; the hired help who came for cropping and harvests also lived with us. There were always at least two men all the time to be totally cared for, as well as beds to be made, rooms kept clean and meals cooked. I baked a cake every day except Sunday.

Our outings were to Mass on Sunday and during the football season to a match if it was local. School picnics became the highlight of the year. Every morning I spent half an hour with the children in the lounge with the radio programme 'Kindergarten of the Air' (with Miss Anne Dreyer and Miss Ruth Fenner). They had their breakfast, washed, combed their hair and were ready for the programme just as if they really were attending kinder-garten. We did all the actions, skipped, marched, clapped and took part in the singing, then sat quietly and listened to the stories. Because my children lived away on a farm in isolation I made sure they did not miss out on anything. Sometimes their cousins on the next farm joined in if they were with us and they would do the same if our children were at their home.

In 1943 I sent for correspondence lessons for our son to begin his schooling. They were interesting and we managed them quite well. I realised that we would have to keep to a strict timetable. We still listened to 'Kindergarten of the Air', so we allowed time off for that and then when he had paper work to do I made sure the other ones did not disturb him by sending them off to gather morning sticks in the bushes surrounding our house. The only trouble we had was when my husband had sheep in the yards and my son used to disappear as soon as he heard them.

'Dad needs me to help him,' was his excuse.

So when a day was wasted in the sheepyards Saturday became a school day. He was not aware of this scheme until his cousins came out one Saturday and they said, 'You don't go to school on Saturday; we know, we go to school now, too'.

But we had to find another farm near a school or send them away to school. Although there often were duststorms there were many more days of beautiful clear sunshine and lovely warmth and we didn't want to leave the Mallee. We found an ideal wheat farm within walking distance of a school; it had a nice home and a huge dam with water laid on to the house and garden; three large tanks, so there would be no shortage of rain water. Never would we have to drink boiled dam water again. We had a real laundry, not a copper in the yard, and the water ran from taps, it did not have to be drawn by a bucket on a rope from a tank used for carting. I think I should have written the word GARDEN in capitals. When I tried to make a garden during the year we had good rainfall my husband assured me I was wasting my time. I was. As soon as it became hot I could not carry enough water and plants drooped and died. Now, with water laid on, a small lawn and a few rose bushes and shrubs already established, I had encouragement.

We would not be so far from neighbours even though we would be no nearer a small town. We would still have to hire help for cropping and harvests, but for the *first time* since we were married, we were just our own family, the two of us with our four little children.

It took my husband quite a while to settle down without his brothers; it made him realise just how hard it had been for me. He was very good, a kind and considerate husband who helped me in every way, but he worked so hard at his farm work there was no time over to help me in the house. To me, this new home was like a new beginning.

It was a new beginning. But 1944 was a total drought: one

of the worst ever experienced in the Mallee. My husband set to work with the tractor, did all the autumn fallowing, then planted the crops — oats, barley and wheat. All we had to do then was wait for them to grow: when the rain came.

It didn't, it blew dust instead. In April the duststorms began; coming over just like a black thundercloud, we had to light lights to see at all inside the house. They said the dust came from South Australia. I am sure it began in the West, gathering from the South as it came, because by the time it reached us there was no hope of seeing through it. Our fallowed paddock came inside the house. The crops grew about three inches high then, after a bad blow, just lay down and died.

There was no grass; we had a horse, a cow and 700 sheep and only one paddock of stubble and a very small haystack already on the property; we were really relying on those crops. We were probably worse off than our neighbours because we had sold all surplus oats and the huge haystack before we moved so could not handfeed the stock; and we had paid the money on the property which was not going to give us one penny that year.

Inviting our neighbour (who was very short of feed for his sheep) to go with us in the car on a weekend, we travelled south to look for grass. There seemed to be plenty on the roadsides as far south as the Ballarat district, at Clunes.

With 700 sheep each, the two men started off the first week in September in a drover's van, with an extra saddle-horse each and their sheep dogs. They trucked everything at the Birchip railway station, rode with them and unloaded at Trawalla, then began droving to Clunes. Before they left I had dreamed that we would not get rain before June.

'We will be home before Christmas,' they said.

Now I had to manage alone; the eldest boy was 7½ years, the youngest child three. I had the car and was glad that I was an experienced driver because when the duststorms were really bad the teacher would keep the children at school until the parents called for them; they would otherwise have become lost in the paddocks. Near the gateway we would wait for a lull in the blow so we could get through safely. One girl rode a horse; she said he could take her home, he would feel the road with his hoofs.

There were about a dozen old ewes left at home because they would not withstand the droving. These kept getting bogged in the mud of the nearly empty dam. I had to pull them out and help them up the bank so I filled a chaff-feeder with water high up on the bank, but they were not used to drinking from anything except the dam so they continued to get bogged. I was lucky I didn't get bogged too. They ate dry burrs and grass seeds and the heaps of horse manure in the horse paddock which the previous owner had kept for his horse teams; they survived.

When the hay ran out I kept the cow alive and well by feeding her the hay used for thatching on the stable and sheds. I would take a pitchfork up onto the top of the stable and after shaking the dirt off, throw the hay to the ground, then soak it in water and add some crude molasses to it to make it palatable. Goodness knows how long ago the hay had been used for thatching.

I also had a lucerne patch in the garden which I kept watered and cut a handful each day for the cow. Because she was short of greenfeed she ate the tops of the boobialla hedge surrounding the garden. When she ate the shoots off the gum trees we could not use her milk because of the strong eucalyptus flavour.

We were still waiting for rain and the dust blew with even the slightest breeze. In November my husband rang up to say that he was able to put the sheep on the railway line from Saturday night until Monday morning and he could get us a little cottage to live in. He would still have to be gone droving on the roads during the week. The next weekend he would come by the early morning train.

We had to take the neighbour's brother to meet the down train to take his place with the sheep — this went through Birchip at 11 p.m. — the up train from Ballarat arrived at 5 a.m. The children and I were pleased to welcome their father, it was the first time he had ever been away from us. All the way from Birchip to our farm every gate was open — no stock to wander in or out, they were either sold or away somewhere on agistment.

One of our neighbouring farmers thought that if he sold his sheep in Melbourne he would have no worries. They sold for less than the freight to send them to Newmarket: he still had to send a cheque for the freight.

The man who was in charge of the channels to fill the dam was very glad of the opportunity of taking our cow while we were away. Their own cows were dry and away on agistment. He was able to get chaff for his channel horses so she would be well fed and he had a family of small children who needed the milk.

We loaded what we needed into a trailer behind the car and arrived at the cottage in time to have everything ready by evening. The little cottage stood under two large pine trees which made a carport for our car. There was very little furniture: we had to bring beds with us. The large wooden box in which I brought our crockery and cooking utensils had to serve as a food cupboard. There was only an open fireplace in the kitchen so I had to learn how to cook with a camp oven. I found a piece of flat tin to put across the bars on the open fire to keep my aluminium saucepans from becoming blackened.

The two men were able to put the sheep in on the Geelong-Ballarat railway line after the last train on Saturday evening and remove them before the first train on Monday morning. There were no Sunday trains. Each week they drove the sheep on a different road then by the weekend were back to the railway line. It rained often in the Ballarat district and was really cold. The children had to wear overcoats to keep dry and warm to go to school: they thought it was wintertime and said, 'It will be nice here when the summer comes.' It was nearly Christmas then.

We spent Christmas with my husband's family who were now in Melbourne doing well with a corner store — groceries, sandwich bar, sweets, drinks and icecream. We had enough petrol to get there but not back, so my husband made up a mixture of petrol, kerosene, methylated spirits, eucalyptus and mothballs. The car went like a 'bomb': it had never performed better.

166

In the new year, 1945, school had begun when we received a telegram from the Sutton school: 'Come back or school will be closed.' So it was back to the dust again. The teacher had already been transferred when we arrived back. We wired the Education Department: 'Ten children waiting for teacher.' Another one was sent.

The state of the house was unbelievable; a hill of sand stood between the back door and garden gate. The dust had to be actually shovelled out of the bath and we swept and swept and swept the floors, at least five times, before we found the lino. There was no lawn, no garden, and the dust still blew: it had covered the open verandah.

The sheep feed on the roads cut out in March. The sheep were brought home to the farm and also a railway truck of huge potatoes too big for the market. We cut them up to feed the sheep.

As I had dreamt, it rained in June: four inches in four days, changing the look of both the countryside and the farmers' faces. My husband put in his second sowing of wheat, barley and oats hoping he would get some returns this year. He kept getting bogged with his tractor. Several times I had to load the boot of the car with mallee stumps to put under the wheels while I pulled him out with the car.

The soil was heavier than the real sandy soil he was used to working, it would set firm after rain. Because the mud balled up under the school children's shoes they tried walking to school barefooted. That wasn't a success; though they washed their feet when they arrived and put on their shoes, the superphosphate in the soil poisoned their feet. At one time there were six feet to be fomented and bandaged.

We had a bumper crop that year, which really made up for the bad drought. The sheep had been saved and we always had our meat to eat. Our cow was returned — the only fat cow in the district. That farm made our finances secure for the rest of our lives. We were glad we didn't give in when things were so black: 'black as a 1944 duststorm'.

This year of 1945 was the year of prosperity; it paid our debts, brought peace in the Pacific and our new baby daughter in September. The four inches of rain in June and good spring rains gave us a good harvest. We were able to settle our debts and buy electrical goods to use with a 32-volt generator plant, which made life much easier for me.

My health had not been good since the baby's birth. I needed an operation but that would have to wait till the baby became more robust. She was very tiny and could not tolerate cow's milk; I had none for her. Lactogen proved unsuitable and Vi Lactogen she could keep down if it was weak enough. She gained an ounce or two a week. The doctor could find nothing abnormal in her digestive system; try giving her scraped raw apple. She loved it; then when she was able to have solid food she began to put on weight. When she was four years old I was able to have the repair operation I should have had after her birth. It was followed by a bout of pneumonia.

No one had told us that after several good seasons the field mice build up to plague proportions: not hundreds or thousands, but millions. The ground becomes a moving sea of grey bodies. The only place they could not invade in our home was on the kitchen table and inside the refrigerator. The kitchen table had round, glossy, enamelled legs that mice could not climb. They invaded every other place in the house; they smelled vile and were ten times worse than any duststorm.

Even though we did not want to use poison we finally had to use it. I was glad I had a wire cot for my baby; the mice ate our hair as we slept. After using the poison, early next morning before the children were awake, I gathered up with a pair of tongs and buckets, hundreds of dead mice from the floors: then washed the floors as a special precaution. Not even photographs could show what a mouse plague is like. Eventually they eat one another.

Apart from the duststorms and mouse plague, we spent many happy years at Culgoa. Only my husband's illness persuaded us to leave — pneumonia, pleurisy, then continuous pain in his chest and leg. He decided to buy a farm in Swan Hill and try grazing since he could no longer use a tractor.

Catherine

Catherine Pearce-Shorten b.1910

WHEN my Scottish family first thought of emigrating to Australia I was about ten years old. During this time of preparation I was sent to stay with my mother's sister at her 'Home Office School' in York, England. I was not at all happy about it. I had never been away from home before and the more I heard about the school the less I liked it. The girls were there for 'Care and Protection' and were trained by house matrons in work suitable for placing them in Service.

I was to go by train from Glasgow to York and the ticket collector would look after me. Most of my luggage was on me.

At York station I was bewildered, it was so big, noisy and dirty. I felt utterly miserable, and even more so when I saw coming towards me, and using her umbrella to clear the way, an older version of my beloved mother. She hurried me to the exit and a taxi.

Listening to Aunt Wilhemina I felt that I was to be here for a much longer time than my parents had said. Words like 'school later on', 'better quality clothing', 'example to the girls in her school'. She was well-off and unmarried.

The following days were spent in visits to the dentist, dressmaker, and shopping or playing with the school dog. I had lessons from my aunt who was a teacher and later, piano

The emigrating MacFarlane family. Catherine in foreground

lessons. I don't know what I was being groomed for, but looking back I realised my aunt was lonely too, and 'putting me to rights' was quite an event for her. I was introduced to her library and questioned about my reading. A few months later I was sent home again. The Macfarlanes were migrating, whatever that might mean: *birds* migrated.

It meant a station cold and foggy, unfamiliar in an autumn evening's dusk; faces appearing and disappearing in a circle to be next to the lucky ones, the 'migrators'; advice and warnings from relatives and friends: 'It's a long way, you'll get awfa' seasick.' And Miss Laidlaw, my schoolteacher, tall and usually forbidding, was wiping an odd tear away, which embarrassed me. I was to 'be a good girl, my mother's right hand, and write often and tell her all about our new life'. I promised, and wished her goodbye. I never wrote to Miss Laidlaw; to my shame, I forgot all about her.

At last we were off, the doors slammed loudly and forms and voices disappeared into the fog. We seemed to hurtle through space on our journey to London. If it wasn't the Flying Scotsman it was a very close relative. Our large old-fashioned trunks were loaded onto the ship at Tilbury Docks and when we found our cabins we wondered how we were going to live in such close quarters for so many weeks. The *Orvieto* was old, creaky and seemed huge to us. In tonnage it was a very small ship. The food was plain and almost always cold.

For many weeks my mother had been packing old underwear and clothing, realising laundering aboard would be difficult. When anything needed changing, it was rolled up into a neat parcel tied with string and thrown overboard. We younger ones would stand behind looking anxiously at near-by passengers and felt as guilty as if my mother was disposing of her offspring, one by one.

Evenings in the tropics my father had to be hounded down to meals. 'Did we consider food to be more important than that sunset, the like of which we would never see again?' It was indeed breathtaking and my father made several attempts to find the trunk with his oils and brushes, but never did. It was a very packed ship.

When it seemed that we had lived on the ship forever and were getting very bored, we awoke one day to the sight of Australian land — we were told. Miles and miles and miles of it. We were very excited and began to pack. Much too soon, it all had to be unpacked again. Then came the day and hour when the gangways went down and we crowded the rail looking for the promised sign 'Mac Family' to be held aloft. It made little difference to us that there were many 'Mac' families aboard, we would surely know our relatives. We did not; we didn't resemble any of them. But we were soon ashore and chattering like a lot of magpies.

We thought Sydney the most breathtaking place and were disappointed we had to continue by train to Brisbane. There, more relatives met us; considering there were eight of us we were treated very lavishly. The men were tall and sunburnt, which is how people overseas think of them. These days even the police seem short, and many who are tall walk with bent shoulders. Not the police! Brisbane seemed more like what we had expected Australia to be. We had seen pictures of houses on high stilts and tin roofs and the people seemed to welcome us even more. We travelled to Cairns by small ship and loved this place instantly. More relatives of relatives. My aunts must all have had large families there were so many at each stop.

From Cairns, the last lap of our journey; we were told that if the weather held we would go by train, but if not, in a fleet of white cars which ran up and down the range. It did rain! People who have visited Kuranda on the Atherton Tableland would know why we could not go by train. We were met in a small township called Malanda by my uncle and cousin who somehow packed us into two utilities and we were on our way to his property a few miles from Malanda. There we met my mother's elder sister and lots more cousins. We stayed here till Father found a house and could settle down to his painting and taking photographs, for which he became quite well-known.

I don't know if we were happy, something was wrong somehow. Although our mother spent a great deal of time looking after the Bush Brothers and the church, she was not well. To this day I can remember the shock of being told that she was incurably ill and could not live long. The most important step in my life was about to begin.

I was seventeen years old when my beloved mother died. This awful happening lives with you forever more. How could she not be there; to tend, to love, to teach, to guide, to count us as we rode through the open gate, 'one, two, three, four, five, six — where's Cathy?' Always last. Not any more to hear her lovely voice ringing out, the beautiful songs, 'Jerusalem', 'Juanita — ask thy soul if we should part', 'My love is like a red, red rose', to hear them, though seldom now, makes my throat constrict still.

People came and went. My elder brothers made plans to leave for the cities of their new country. My sister went to work in a nursing home. Archie was to go to boarding school. But what was to happen to me? I dreaded the future. No more sing-songs round the piano. No more catching sulphur-crested cockatoos with a horse hair. No more riding through the bush, the dogs running alongside. No more anything; and my father would probably send me to his own church, which for me seemed cold and forbidding after the warm and familiar C. of E. A cold and empty world as Archie, too, departed in the chill of a very early morning.

Then my father showed me a letter, from my aunt in England. She welcomed me to come and stay with her for as long as I cared. I felt very unhappy. I did not want to go. It didn't occur to me that I had any say in the matter. I would miss everything familiar; the tropical sun, the rain forests with the strange birds and the flashing green wings. I had grown used to freedom.

Aboard the *Oronsay* the purser took charge of my passport, my keys and my money. For many days I was so homesick I stayed on my bunk and feigned sea-sickness. We ran into deep fog. The ship slowed to a crawl and sounded her fog horn constantly. The captain asked us to kneel on the deck and pray. He didn't know where we were and it was possible we might collide with another ship. I knew about fog. I was born in one, in cold bleak Scotland when, I was told, the doctor had difficulty finding the street and the house. It would clear soon.

As time surely passes, which is hard to believe at times, the day of our arrival dawned. I waited for my aunt who came late and looking anxious. A last look at the ship. Would I go back one day? Aunt's umbrella, as usual, was at the ready. She was a highly intelligent woman, a graduate of St Andrew's University and I knew I would be taken in hand again.

'When did I last visit the dentist?' I thought of the one and only dentist in Malanda, getting on in years, who did not like drilling teeth and much preferred to pull them out. Notes made in a huge diary: check-up by school doctor, visit dentist, get rid of all present wardrobe and be fitted with new outfit, etc., etc. I should have been pleased, it was all for my own good, but I was quite happy with my state of health and decayed teeth, not to mention my 'new clothes' for the journey. I had a sudden thought and a giggle. Would my aunt roll my things into a bundle and leave them, one dark night, on the common? Which is exactly what she did!

Portsmouth, England, 1939

The handle of the spade was cold. I had a blister on my thumb and my back ached. We were filling sandbags from the beach and stacking them to be collected. From right inside I felt tired and weary.

I looked across the grey sullen sea. What a long way away my family seemed, on the other side of the world. What were they doing? Were my four brothers already in uniform? My father, getting on in years, would be with my sister and family. They would be worried about me, but it would not be for long, God willing. At least they were in sunny Queensland, and safe.

The last sandbag filled, I reported, had my name ticked off and quickly cycled home; past the rolls of barbed wire, the shelters being erected in the streets and manned by wardens; past the new signs 'Don't throw anything away — everything is useful' and 'Walls have ears — don't talk loudly.'

My aunt had bought a house in Devonshire Avenue only eighteen months ago. And now, after her long long years of devoted work, she was stricken with cancer. I prayed the air raids would never happen. How would I carry her down two flights of stairs to the air raid shelter in the garden?

I listened outside my aunt's door; all seemed to be quiet. I decided I'd earned a cup of tea. Then I saw the morning mail on the hall table. Bills, a letter from Australia, and a buff-coloured envelope stamped OHMS. As I opened that, I had a feeling, here was the answer to my feeling of uneasiness all morning. It was. 'Report to Queen Alexandra Hospital in future local casualty clearing station for troops. You will be required full time. Take evidence of your nursing experience. Arrangements for fitting of Civil Nursing Reserve uniform to be forwarded in due course.'

But how could I? My aunt was sixty-five years old, upstairs, dying of cancer of the lungs. She would not even have any help or medication, and the doctor had given up trying. He would just have to help me tell the Ministry I couldn't work full time. I was working full time already, with the help of a woman who, herself, would be called up soon for other work.

It was to no avail. I was informed that arrangements would be made, through our doctor, for Miss Custance to be admitted to a nursing home. I was to report to the Matron-in-chief who would give me all instructions. Well, we must indeed be at war, for such high-handedness.

As it happened, the patients in the nursing homes were all sent to reception areas and the Royal Portsmouth Hospital was full — so we just had to manage.

It was not so bad at the start. I cycled up the long distance to the hospital and was given instructions regarding duties, ward, etc. The building was large and old and not equipped for the sort of work that lay ahead of us. We made beds, covered sandbags (for fractured limbs) checked medicine cupboards and got to know each other. The charge sister was entirely responsible, I came next, then two Red Cross nurses and a Nursing Auxiliary (Naughty Annies, the troops called them, these young and wonderful helpers).

When I was relieved by my opposite number I would cycle home as quickly as was safe, usually after our helping neighbour had gone, and I would creep upstairs, not knowing what I was going to find. The evening was spent making my aunt comfortable, or as comfortable as it was possible for her to be. She had never smoked in her life, was years ahead of her time in her attitude to correct food, and she drank only barley water. So why, why had this to happen?

After many days of weary work at both ends, my aunt died on 28 April, her birthday. I was given a few days leave to arrange everything. I put up blackout curtains which were compulsory. I was now quite alone. I realised how much I had depended on my aunt and how strong her influence had been. I wished I could go home.

Life was rapidly changing in England, and the change calmly accepted. Portsmouth was preparing its own defences and beaches were now out of bounds, with seemingly never-ending mounds of barbed wire, and the parks were being dug up for shelters. Things became scarce and expensive. More and more signs went up. At the hospital there was a feeling of ominous quiet.

We had long briefing sessions. 'We would be expected to sign the Official Secrets Act. We could not live at the hospital but must try to live as near as possible. We should receive a living-out allowance and must find our own transport. Gas masks should be carried at all times, and identity cards always at hand. It was regretted that tin helmets were in short supply. And we should, in winter, state our names and duties before entering the main gate. Report again tomorrow.'

I was beginning to find it very tiresome, going to and fro each day between the hospital and my now, very lonely, home. The blackout curtains were always down and I didn't have time for shopping. I didn't like being alone, and usually slept or tried to keep my bicycle in good running order. I knew I would find it hard to get parts.

At the hospital we were 'ready'. We nurses called each other by our surnames, I got 'Mac' and my best friend was Duffy, a theatre staff-nurse, always smelling of anaesthetic, very pretty, good at her job and the most untidy person I had ever met. One evening she asked me if I would go into Portsmouth with her after we finished work, as she had volunteered to sell cups of coffee for troops at the barracks' church hall. I was on the verge of saying I was too tired and then I thought of the dark, lonely house, and said yes.

We relieved some others and were shown around; jokes were made about finding me a box to stand on or I would not be able to lift the jugs. Duffy was on 'washing up' (almost asleep on her feet) and I passed the full cups to the men behind the counter.

'Some Enchanted Evening' from the musical *South Pacific* had not been composed or written then. I had never believed that you could see someone, across a crowded room, a complete stranger, and know at once that that person was the one, the only one, that would ever matter to you. But it did happen.

I used to blush easily and I was annoyed with myself that

the soldier had noticed my red face and spilling tea. I thought that no-one could look like that and be an ordinary person. He was blonde, with very blue eyes, tall, and so handsome. He looked rather young, though, and possibly not married. Everything about me suddenly seemed different. The wet counter was beautiful, the noisy chatter and the clanking of cups became scarcely noticeable. I loved him in that instant. His name was Terry.

He slowly walked over to me and asked for another cup of coffee. I could not look directly at him. Had I seemed 'flighty'? I gave him his drink and turned to serve others, but at going-home time I knew he would be waiting at the door. Duffy had gone off on one of her dates.

Terry took it for granted, without words, that we both knew what had happened. He told me about himself. He came from East Anglia. He lived with, and had been brought up by his grandparents. His father had been killed in the First World War at the age of twenty-one. He was six years younger than I. That's that, I thought; he would not bother any more when he knew I was older. When he did know, he laughed. If it didn't matter to me, it certainly didn't matter to him.

I forgot all about it and life suddenly seemed worth living. The brooding thought, back in my mind not dazed with this glorious feeling, tried to remind me that he must go, sometime. We could not discuss it. He was not permitted to and I was not to ask. What he did do, was suggest in a roundabout way, that when the time came he would say, 'My grandmother is knitting me another pair of socks.' I would know then that he might come to our next meeting, or not come at all — ever.

We tried not to let this intrude and our daily tasks seemed lighter at the thought that we could spend even a little time together. One evening Terry asked me if I would marry him, if and when he returned. We could, he said, be married at once, but he thought that would not be fair to me. I would meet hundreds of troops and they would all want to marry me!

I didn't need time to make up my mind. He was all that I

ever could have wanted; kind, considerate, brave, affectionate, full of fervour and love for his country — forgetting what love for his country had cost his young father who never even got to see his baby son. I assured him I would wait for however long it took and I would write as I felt, even though the eyes of the censor would read the words before his. A few nights later I stood at the same spot, waiting, but he did not come.

I tried to work harder, if that was possible. Duffy left her 'digs' to come down to Southsea to keep me company. That was a big help. At least we tried to get a meal together and have some sort of social life. Everything was getting scarce. Tins of Spam became a luxury and were nicknamed 'England's last hope'. We had some banana essence and found that if you added it to mashed parsnip it made a nice sweet. We were issued with clothes-rationing books. I didn't need much, being in uniform most of the time and wearing warm navy-blue overalls with short fur-lined boots at other times.

Time moved slowly and I couldn't get home quickly enough for the postman. If anyone thinks they have read most of the famous great loveletters, they have never read Terry's! Duffy kept me busy at home. She tried to copy my 'tidy ways' but eventually gave up. Life is too short to be so tidy, she said.

With Dunkirk, we became a clearing station. All leave was cancelled and lists went up in the main hall showing where we had been placed for immediate duty. I had some very harrowing experiences during the long war, some dreadful, some shattering, some frightful, but I think the Dunkirk admission was the worst. To my dismay, I was posted at the front entrance with two officer surgeons. At a nearby door, another team was waiting.

As the stretcher bearers ran towards the oncoming ambulances and brought the first patient over, I wanted to be sick. I also wanted to hold on to the stretcher, but already the second one was waiting. His injuries were so bad that the field doctor had applied a temporary plaster and instructions were written there. His 'dog tag' (identity disk) was badly twisted. I looked at the young doctor. A muscle in his jaw was twitching and as he caught my eye there was a swift look of 'Don't let me down, I need all the help I can get.' I pulled myself together. I remembered our Medical Officer's talks: 'It will be worse than awful but all you can do is pull a shutter down.' I did that, but I can still see those terrible injuries and the face covered, too awful to be exposed.

Came one stretcher, and the doctor's jaw again twitching; he said 'Moribund' and a young person was wheeled to a near-by darkened ward, to die. A padre hovered in the shadows.

I cried within myself. Dear God, can this really be true? It seemed as though we had looked down on shattered bodies for days. In fact we were not asked to endure it for too long and were replaced. We hurried to the 'head ward' where the men with head injuries were all together. There seemed to be panic and disorder everywhere. Each man's boots, and his equipment if he had any, were placed under his bed. The beds were far too close together but even then, stretchers were on the floor in the corridor. Orders came: Get the least injured ready for immediate evacuation to a reception area. This lightened the load a little, although it seemed cruel to be getting rid of badly wounded men.

In the event, they were the lucky ones. The Germans paid us a visit and the guns were in action most of the night. We could not ask to go off duty. Mattresses were provided below the wards. Damp and horrible. We ate behind the ward kitchen door. Anything provided for a patient that had not been touched was good enough for us. We had forgotten, most of us, what nice meals were like. The people were magnificent; they went to the shelters carrying bedding and baskets with any sort of food obtainable. The water mains had a direct hit and people had to queue with pails and jugs for water.

The first raid on Portsmouth was on 11 July 1940. Eighteen persons were killed and eighty injured. To write about it, in truth, is very difficult. I would have to say, I was terrified, and wanted to make for the cellars whilst being rooted to the spot. We had no patients at this time, fortunately, but the standing by, waiting, had been nerve wracking. Now here at last, 'they' had come, pouring down their bombs on helpless civilians who had the misfortune to live in a front line naval city.

The wail of the warning siren, not 'testing' this time, had made us look at each other in consternation. This was it. We had to show what we were made of now. The anti-aircraft guns made short spasmodic blasts; search lights moved to and fro across the sky to aid them. The sickening thud of high explosive in the distance made us creep further into the ward, away from the glare.

Big fires sprang up and made the work of the rescue teams hard and dangerous. One of the orderlies wheeled several chairs into the ward. He was full of 'news'. 'They' had dropped a bomb right into a big gasholder and four enemy aircraft had been shot down; London was burning and we were preparing for many casualties.

Hours later the All Clear siren gave forth its heart-warming sound. We were sent out in ambulances to help where it was needed. Later, as I made my way home, I realised I would not be able to stay there much longer. It was too dangerous. The rubble began to spread and without lights it was a strain. Houses were being sold at giveaway prices. Most of the young and the elderly had been sent away. Each person had a job to do. Land Army, Factories, Army, Navy, Air Force, Women's Volunteer Service, Red Cross, 'Dad's Army', Wardens, Fire Brigades and many others were mobilised for total war effort.

I applied for living accommodation closer to the hospital and closed the house. It is a marvel, looking back, to realise that hundreds of homes were left like this, but never any reports of looting or theft. I locked up and wiped away the writing on the front gate '2 persons in this house' which had been crossed out to '1'. It helped the people looking for victims, to know how many there should have been.

The second big raid resulted in widespread damage. In twenty minutes, twenty-five bombers severely punished Portsmouth and the Isle of Wight. Thirteen people were killed and over a hundred injured. An air-raid shelter was hit by a bomb while packed with people. They were able to crawl out later when wardens made an escape hole. As time went on the raids became constant and heavy. Behind the hospital an army fort, full of troops, made us a convenient target. Why not put us both out of action?

We were short of supplies, short of help; the doctors and staff were now at sea or in the Middle East. Archie, my brother in the 9th Division AIF was taken prisoner in North Africa. Ronald was with the 7th Division. Terry was in the 8th Army and later trapped with the 'Rats' in Tobruk.

Bombs were getting closer to my Devonshire Avenue house and I was advised to sell. I hated doing it. The furniture, all from Harrogate antique shops, was auctioned. A valuable Ming fruit dish was sold for £3. The four-bedroomed house, with its walled garden and teeming memories, was sold for £1,200. I was very upset and wrote to my father and sister. The boys were so scattered. My father was ill with worry and knew how I must feel. Terry's letters were a great comfort. And he was all right!

As winter wore on life became more difficult. Women in the Army, Navy or Air Force were well looked after. Nurses were never considered for some strange reason and we had to be grateful if we were given so much as a tin of Nivea (face cream) in exchange for something else.

As we became accustomed to procedure, life on the wards became easier. I was sent one day to the 'Limb Ward'. Each patient had had an amputation and it was our job to try and prepare the stump for an artificial limb. The patients were sent away as the beds were to be prepared for yet more unlucky troops.

The night of the Guildhall fire and its destruction angered the people more than anything else. The Guildhall was the pride and inspiration of the city. The Luftwaffe showered it with incendiary bombs till it caught fire and then a high explosive bomb hit the roof, which finally fell in. Three hundred raiders dropped 25,000 incendiaries and high explosive bombs and at one time twenty-eight major fires were burning. There were 171 people killed, 430 injured and 3,000 persons were left homeless. Worse was to come; the main General Hospital and the Ear, Nose and Throat Hospital were badly bombed. The patients of course had to come to us. We were now nursing troops (of both sexes) and civilians who were mostly young or old. People forgot the stern rule — do not take shelter under stairs or near greenhouses (in gardens). Injuries were very severe when large house beams collapsed or glass was shattered by bomb blast. I was to spend many hours with forceps, extracting glass which comes to the surface. One of my worst assignments was 'specialing' a young mother, blinded, and whose baby had been killed. I was drained mentally and physically and at one stage held on to the roller towel behind the kitchen door, feeling that I could not go on any longer. Eventually the patients were moved to Oxford.

More preparation, cleaning up, replenishing and a good night's sleep. We had a severe raid one evening which brought mostly bomb-blast damage, telling us that someone else must be getting the brunt. Was it Southampton again?

Next morning twelve of us were told to report to the Matron-in-chief. We were to pack extra uniforms (no mention of overnight wear!) and be ready to board transport at so-many hours. The army vehicle took the road to the ferry for the Isle of Wight. So that's where the trouble had been, and obviously enough of it for them to take twelve of us from our own constant target and busy station.

We chatted among ourselves. Did someone want a toothbrush? She had packed two, just in case. Someone else mentioned her last holiday on the Isle, a much liked resort. What had they done to it? As we left the ferry we were joined by an army unit in the care of a very young captain. The men lined up and we waited close by for our instructions. I looked round and saw the boxes being unloaded. It was ammunition. The captain looked tired, so young but so old. It was, as for most of us, a case of too much responsibility.

They were about to load the boxes on to trucks when the Alert siren blew. At once, the captain ordered us to lie flat on the pier. We heard 'Jerry' go over and come back again from the mainland. He kept circling round and I thought about what might happen if he dropped a bomb near us — and all that ammunition. I looked through the space between the two boards I was lying on. Underneath, the water was gently lapping against the quayside. Barnacles covered every inch of rock. There was a lovely smell of seaweed and reminders of sand castles. I lifted my chin slightly and saw the captain looking at his men, packs on their backs, big heavy boots, battle dress, and mostly so young. At least they had tin helmets.

The plane circled and came back. I thought about my family in far North Queensland. What were they doing, so far from the ferry on the Isle of Wight? One of my colleagues looked at me, and winked. I gave her a swift grin. She was as brave as a lion. Her name was Barrett and she was a rebel. Probably 'arrived' before her time! The wink stopped me from expecting the worst. It was getting very uncomfortable lying face down and when there had been quiet for a long period the officer gave permission to sit up. When the All Clear sounded a look of enormous relief swept his face. We had been sitting ducks amidst the boxes of explosives. The men were marched off to transport and at the rear, the captain turned, smiled, and said, 'Wherever you are going, good luck, Nurses.'

To our concern we were then separated and I went, alone, to Ryde General Hospital. I was sent to help in a ward of civilians, and at night time assumed I would be told where to sleep. Instead, I was told to report to a room with one patient. I was so weary I faltered, and sat down on a chair for a few moments, then went into the room. Two male nurses were ready to leave and I looked at them in disbelief.

I read the report handed to me. The patient was a police sergeant who had been in a building which had collapsed. He was under heavy sedation. The room was in a dreadful state. When I looked hard at the head nurse he said, 'He is frantic when he comes round. He doesn't know who he is, where he is or what's happened. Just keep him sedated.' 'I'm sorry,' he added, 'there's no-one to help or relieve you, till 8 a.m.'

I sat down, unable to accept that I would have to manage

this huge man alone, till morning. I couldn't, I was too tired. I just wanted to crawl away, away from war, from noise, from blood, from screams, from work. I suddenly thought of Barrett. Where had they sent her? Wherever she was, she would not be cowering, feeling sorry for herself, I pulled myself together. Whatever had to be done must be done.

The men left. I pressed the bell to the office several times. There was no answer. I made sure of my instructions. I saw the bars at the end of the bed. They were twisted, and the patient was tied in his cot. I tidied the room quietly, lowered the light, prepared a sitting place by the bed, and sat down.

Before long, my patient stirred and started muttering. He then became violent and struck out in all directions. What could I do? He could really hurt himself, and me, and I knew there was no help. The place was too crowded for safety and there could be a raid at any moment. I read his name again — Patrick Cooper. That meant he was probably called Paddy.

I undid his pyjama coat and saw what I had hoped was there. He was a Catholic and besides his tag he had his Cross. I felt under the pillow and blessed the nurses. They had put his rosary near him. For the rest of the night, till dawn when I was relieved, Paddy said his Rosary, and I managed.

I left the ward and was allowed two hours sleep. During the day I called to see how Paddy was doing. He had already gone to the mainland for surgery. A young policeman packing his bags told me that he had heard a rumour — 'The Jerries tried to land on the Island last night, at the back, they were all drowned in oil covered water.' I did not believe this, but I heard it again and although it was kept very quiet, I guessed now why the soldiers and ammunition came to the island on the same ferry. We stayed four nights and were then returned to our own stations.

I had little time to think of my own affairs during the months and years but a letter from Terry, who had arrived at El Alamein, made me realise that I was a real person and that if we were lucky, we also had a future. Terry asked me to marry him when he came home and I wrote back at once and told him 'Yes, please!'

At the beginning of June 1944 we had orders to empty the beds and prepare. Prepare for what? Long wards, empty beds, stretchers in the hall, sand bags, drug cupboards re-stocked; wheelchairs; Moribund reopened. Oh no, not again. Long talks. Reminders; walls have ears. Injections for this and that. Quinine. 6 June and it was here. 'D-Day'.

News of the actual landing was scarce. We knew that many had drowned or were killed by the Nazis or taken prisoner. We waited. We were ready and there it was all over again, too little of everything. I had no particular ward, I was a 'runner', going wherever they desperately needed help. The wounded arrived one after the other in the wards; boots, helmets, papers, quickly having to be sorted out. Dress their wounds, give them food if allowed, make as comfortable as possible, and await evacuation orders.

I was sent to a ward outside the main building. Evacuate and prepare ward. Orders on the desk. Only one or two patients were left. I went to the nearest one. He was about twenty-three. He smiled at me and I smiled back. 'Hullo. What are you doing here all by yourself?' He told me he was waiting for me — had been waiting for years. What kept me?

'Oh, a cheeky one,' I thought. Well I would get a wheel-chair and take him to join the others at the front, waiting for the ambulances.

I looked for a chair but there wasn't one and no sign of any nursing staff. I gathered up his papers without looking at them, there wasn't time.

'Well, Bob, off we go. Where are your boots?'

'Who needs boots?' he said, and whipping back the blanket he displayed two small stumps. He had no legs.

'I'm sorry, Bob.'

Why shouldn't I scream. It's not fair, it's just not fair.

He looked up and said, 'Now you have to carry me.' 'I'm not heavy,' he added.

I carried him and put up with his antics on the way to the

185

ambulance. What could happen? If I came face to face with some high ranking person or MIC (Matron in charge), I could only plead with my eyes — till later. He turned my cap back to front and held on much too tightly, making a joke of everything. He told me his other name was Edwards.

I saw the ward orderly and called out to him. Edwards quickly kissed me and said, 'Goodbye, Nursie.' I had become very used to most things by this time, but always the wretched 'lump' would come, to make me speechless . . .

Then Hitler released the 'Doodlebugs' on us; the secret weapons, V 1 and V 2. If we thought high explosives were bad, the 'Vs' were shocking. They killed 5,000 people in the first London raid and then came on to Portsmouth. They killed 8,000 people. The Germans bombed Portsmouth up until May 1945.

At this time my back was giving me trouble. Never strong since my days at the Royal Seabathing Hospital, the war years had finished the job. I was told after X-rays I was unfit for further ward duties, to take a week's rest and report for duty in the Department of the Ministry of Pensions. Just like that. Poor old horse — no further use. I handed in my uniform and was given the Defence medal.

I disliked office work and, to rub salt in, I was put in charge of paying the funeral expenses of people killed in the Blitz. I had letters from Terry. Would I arrange for us to be married in church? I was able to be in church for the bans to be called; it seemed strange to be free at weekends. Archie was now free and instead of returning to Australia with his mates, he would come and give me away. I was so happy. My two men would be there. The church was at Wymering and called 'Wymering-cum-Widley'; very very old, small, with beautiful stained glass windows.

I was finding the days long and lonely in my new work. The staff had all come from Reading, the 'big works', and didn't like Portsmouth. I missed my own work and the feeling of being needed. Then a letter came from Terry, it was posted in the UK. So he was home! There might be a future for us after all.

Despite weeks and weeks and hours and hours of time off due to me I had to approach the Senior almost on bended knee, to ask for one day off to go to London. How long had Terry been in the Middle East? Four and a half years, sir. (In all he was in the Army for over six years and on Anzac Day wears the Africa Star with 8th Army clasp, the Italy Star, the 1939-1945 Star, the Oak Leaf (Mentioned in Despatches), the Tobruk Siege Medal with Small Rat.) I was given the day off.

In London, on Waterloo station, I sat and watched the huge clock for hours and hours. It had been so long; had I changed much? What had his experiences done to him? As the time drew near I could hardly bear it. When the train pulled in I wanted to race madly down the platform.

In the crowd I could not see him, but when I did and he saw me coming, we both ran and neither of us could speak. At last he stepped back and looked at me. We sat on a seat in the station and talked and talked and talked. We arranged our wedding, and I had to bear the news that he would not be demobbed for a while yet, he would be at Chatham in Kent. I could go there, if I could get time off, after we were married. From time to time we went and bought the famed 'station tea', strong and sweet. But we did not notice it. We talked all night and after washing and brushing up, Terry caught his train and I caught mine and went straight to the office.

Everyone noticed the difference in me. I could cope with anything now. Terry was as wonderful as I remembered him, all that time ago. Older in many ways, weather-beaten, he was disinclined to talk about his experiences and belittled his Mention in Despatches and the report on his UK Arrival Card, 'This man has an exemplary character.' He has indeed. He can take a lengthy period removing a small insect from inside the house to put it down gently outside in the garden. What could it have been like 'following up' with the 8th Army and being dug in at Tobruk?

At long last Archie came with a big Australian hat and a

happy smile. What had it been like for him, a prisoner of war for 4½ years, a lad from the outdoors in Queensland, who could ride any horse, swim like a fish and played all sports?

On 1 June 1945 we were married at the old church and Archie gave me away. So many people came and we were given some handsome gifts. Two dear friends gave us return tickets to Loch Lomond and everyone put in with clothing coupons for me to get a wedding gown and going-away outfit. I went up to Liberty's in London and had a big splurge. I was so happy.

The war at last was over; cheering and flag waving and crowds with wan faces flushed in relief. Once a year, for two silent minutes, there is remembrance for those who died. They should be remembered every day, in gratitude.

Terry and I sailed for Australia on the troopship *Asturias*. It cost us each £200, to share a cabin with seven others. There were over 500 children aboard ship. Most of the mothers, brides of Australian servicemen, looked so young. It seemed a lot of money to pay for the 'privileges' we were to have. It was still a troopship and we were under the control of the Australian Government. Our luggage had to be left out in

The wedding group

the corridor. The ship travelled via the Cape of Good Hope and a nerve-wracking experience it was. The captain threatened to turn back if the mothers did not control their children who were climbing onto the covered lifeboats. Prams were left on deck, rolling to and fro, and babies fell from cabin bunks. In Capetown, hordes of hungry British migrants cleaned up city cafés and restaurants like locusts. They hadn't seen good food for a long, long time.

After a lifetime of days at sea, of years of war, of nursing years before that, I was again in Cairns, where with racing heart and butterfly stomach I looked around for my family. It was a shock to see my father and sister looking so much older, but then, they all thought that about me. I felt tearful and drained and tired as we piled into my brother-in-law's car to take us to their home in Atherton. What was in front of us now? Could Terry find work here? Would we be homesick?

But as usual, something turns up, which you had never thought about. We met, at a party, an old friend of the family. He offered Terry a job in his business, which seemed a bit of everything; selling real estate, farm equipment, spares, and even rounding up brumbies. It was in Malanda!

Memories came back; my dear mother and my family as we all were; riding bare back to the state school; learning how to kill a snake with a stick; and my teacher Mr Reeves telling me that one day I would write an article. Is this an 'article'? For me it is a glorious outlet because it is happening.

Terry commenced his work and I began to explore the country round the town for some land on which we could build. How easy it was then; so much of it, and so cheap.

Eventually we found a spot, high on the hill and near a rain forest where we could hear the birds. Our bank manager told us we could buy a house very cheaply from a nearby 'dead' mining town. We went out to the site and it was great fun going from one house to the other, trying to pick the best. Really, they were much of a muchness. It came as something of a shock when I realised the house first had to be demolished. But of course, how else could it get to the spot on the hill we had found. The agent told us he could not give us a precise date for delivering the house as the people who owned the huge haulage truck were very busy. However, we were assured it would be as soon as possible.

It did come, on one very hot day. I was in the shower and a murmur of excitement came from the street below. What could it be? Wrapped in my bath towel I peeped over the verandah rail. What a sight to behold!

I stood transfixed in my two puddles of water, as the most enormous trailer I had ever seen came slowly round the corner. Mounted high in piles of timber, doors, walls, windows and tin roof was our house. Even the dunny was packed at the back. I could feel my spirits dropping with the drips to the floor. How could that mess ever resemble a respectable, comfortable home with nice furniture and curtains?

After dinner we went up to our plot to see what had happened. The mess had all been dumped on the ground, and the men were just moving off. Apparently we didn't even have to sign for it. We sat down on the wall of the kitchen and gazed despairingly at each other.

Well, we would wait and meet each problem as it came. During the next week we contacted the builders, but it seemed they were fully booked for about the next five weeks and then they might start, depending on the Wet!

Almost to the day, the rains began, and poured steadily down, day after day, week after week, drumming incessantly on the tin roof. And after inspecting our 'pile of timber' we felt that it would never happen. Even the wet season has to end however, and one morning we awoke to find the sun shining and the red muddy roads with deep wheel tracks, glistening in the bright light.

More urgent contact with the builder. Yes, they were now ready to start (what had they been doing all this time I wondered) tomorrow morning early.

After a quick consultation we both decided we would leave it to them and not be hovering around like nervous butterflies. After two or three days of humid conditions we felt that the timber would eventually dry out and began to be a little more optimistic.

We were warned by many 'experts' lounging around the hotel, that our builders were no good — just bush builders, self-taught — only in more colourful language. We did not care at that time. All we wanted was to see our house standing upright.

We spent our weekends walking slowly round but felt that the imperfections were few. Then at last! It was complete. Roof on, tin caps to stop the termites and a large new water tank. Delighted, we looked round to see that we were even fenced off from our neighbours. All the transaction seemed to be happening outside, which I thought was strange, but it did not take very long and we shook hands with the men and left them, to see our home at last.

We were almost breathless with excitement, opening the front door, eager to start deciding where the furniture would go. It was short lived. We looked up at the ceiling, tongued and grooved — and groaned aloud. There growing in the red soil, all over the room, were weeds and flowers. It was unbelievable. We remembered then, the warnings about 'bush carpenters'.

For the first time we were not just dismayed, but really angry. They could at least have brushed the soil off before nailing up, thus saving many hours of hard work. We borrowed steps and planks and Terry had to lay on his back on a plank, with brushes tied to his feet and move them backwards and forwards till the dirt fell on paint cloths below. When most of it was off we hosed the ceiling (after all, what did a little more water matter).

We cleaned the windows, painted the floors and gathered wood for the stove, which I had already examined with a sinking heart. The furniture (much too good for the house) arrived and we moved in. Well, if it wasn't perfect at least it was our own, and our feelings weren't too hurt when the Chinese gardener who came once a week with vegetables, said, 'You live in funnee house'!

In our spare time we cleared the garden at the back, often

with avid visitors watching: a line of kookaburras. But watching Terry I felt this was not what he wanted although not for the world would he have me think so. I thought about it a great deal. My family in Atherton had their own interests and did not see much of us anyway. I had been away so long. Terry's job was easy and often dull.

I began to pretend I was not very happy and longed to return to the city. A happier-looking Terry said, 'Are you sure?' and we hugged each other. So we sold the funny house and said goodbye to the bush and left to seek our fortunes in Brisbane.

Yvonne

Yvonne Banfield b.1909

MY mother was a very small person but what she lacked in size she made up in courage and determination. Always ready to help anyone in trouble she was sometimes appreciated and often taken for granted, but she was never deterred. I would often say, 'Why do you bother with those people?' to which she would simply reply, 'Some day I will get my reward in heaven.'

My answer to that was, 'It would be nice to get a little down here.'

My mum had a great love and understanding of animals, large and small. She had a natural gift with sick ones and they responded to her without fear and seemed to have an instinctive knowledge that she would help them. Over the years I saw her helping numerous cats, dogs and cows that had trouble having their babies and she never lost one little kitten, puppy, calf or a mum.

The neighbours from near and far brought their animals to her and she would always help them but never accept payment. Some of the animals might have broken bones, sores that had become flyblown; cows that had an empaction would have to be given a drench of:

one pound of epsom salts
one tin treacle
two tablespoons of bi-carbonate soda.

This she dissolved in a quart of boiling water, allowed to cool then poured into a beer bottle. She would hold the animal's head up and place the neck of the bottle in the side of its mouth, then pour the liquid slowly down its throat. It all had to be done very carefully so as not to let the liquid go down the wrong way and onto the lungs or pneumonia would set in. In those days there were no antibiotics available and most home treatments were accompanied with lots of love and reassurance for the patient.

I have known my mum to sit up all night with a sick animal, making it comfortable with straw and keeping it covered with rugs and bags. If it had a fever she would keep giving it buckets of cold water to help take the temperature down and she had to make sure it did not throw its head around as that is what very sick animals do and they can severely injure themselves.

In 1905 my parents had bought thirteen acres of land in Rosanna, ten miles from the Melbourne GPO. It was then considered to be out in the never-never; no motor cars, only horse-drawn cabs, jinkers, spring carts, wagons. Eventually they decided to build a house on the front part of the block but its completion was delayed by a builders' strike which lasted for about nine months. Then the great day came for us to move in.

I remember arriving at Heidelberg station in a steam train, with loads of trunks and hat boxes, then climbing into a horse-drawn cab which was entered by a step at the back and had a seat on either side. We set off, clip clop, down the main street with its fine little shops and Rank's hay and corn store on the corner (now it is a restaurant — Salzberg Lodge). There were two funeral parlours, two banks, a bakery, a saddlery, and Rouche's timber yard where the old whistle blew at 8 a.m., noon and 5 p.m. There was Clinton's bike shop, the post office and the Sir Henry Barkly Hotel, and further down the blacksmith's shop and forge shaded by an enormous oak tree. I can still hear the striking of the anvil and the pumping of the bellows. As we turned into Rosanna Road the big old clock at the Austin Hospital (for Cancer and Incurable Diseases as it was known then) started to strike. It

Yvonne with parents

was the most mournful sound one could imagine.

As we came to the corner of Lower Plenty and Rosanna Roads I saw this big white cyclone gate and my father waiting to open for us. I vividly remember he was dressed in dark trousers, Assam silk coat and beautiful hand-made tan shoes, panama hat and a large silk handkerchief around his neck.

Rosanna is so changed now. There were, in those days, only about twenty houses spread around in acres and acres of open paddocks. The roads were un-named and un-made, some just dirt tracks. The main roads were formed and covered with blue metal broken up with a big sledge hammer by a little old man with a beard who wore bow-yangs. His name was Paddy Cashin. He may not have been old, just bent with that job. There were no footpaths, just grassy tracks; cows and horses roamed at will, our own included.

We had candle and kerosene lighting, ice chest, wood stove, wood copper for washing and open fireplaces in every room. We made our own butter and had fowls and chickens everywhere. There were three steam trains up and three down per day and it took an hour to get in to Princes Bridge, Melbourne.

In the summertime it was lovely to see and smell the fruit wagons going in to market from Hurstbridge and Diamond Creek at about 8 o'clock of an evening. All the local children, about six of us, used to jump on the back of the wagon and help ourselves to the fruit. Next morning the wagons would pass our place on their way home. The driver would be sound asleep and the old horses would take them home safely.

I was just turned thirteen years old when my father, walking to the Rosanna station, was hit from behind by a bolting horse harnessed to a fish cart. The memory of that day is still fresh in my mind. It was 28 August 1923, and the wind was blowing at 68 miles per hour.

Mum was working in the kitchen and I was practising five-finger exercises on the piano when I heard a knock at the front door, and there was the local butcher standing on the mat. He said to me, 'Your father has met with an accident and some people are bringing him home.'

I rushed out to tell Mum. By this time the very kind people had pulled up at our back door in a tiny 'baby runabout' car as they were called in those days. We helped carry my father into the bedroom and a doctor was called. When he arrived he said there was nothing he could do but get him to the hospital as soon as possible. But my father died before anything could be done for him.

Next morning I was terribly upset to see my poor mother. She had lovely brown hair, but with the shock of my father's death it had turned completely white. It took many months but eventually it went back to its natural colour.

I seemed to grow up overnight. My mother leant very heavily on me and looked to me to take my father's place, and also to be a daughter. The next few years were very hard; we didn't have much money but somehow we managed. I met a wonderful young man and we married, but the Depression was creeping on. It made a great difference in our lives, and as I look back, made better people of us. It was a challenge to survive.

We had started farming, so with the eggs, vegetables, milk and butter we were able to get three meals a day. There were unpaid bills and sleepless nights wondering where the money was coming from to pay them. We made do with things our relatives had cast off, patching and mending until there was hardly anything to hold the garment together. We used to put cardboard and brown paper in our shoes when the soles were getting thin.

Although times were so hard we also had our joys. Our little family, one boy and one girl and our own deep love for each other made life very much worth living in those days.

Then my husband was offered a job at Strattons Flour Mill, Victoria Park, lumping bags of wheat from the railway siding to the huge silos. It was very hard work and the wages £4 12s per week, but it was a fortune to us. The freeway now runs over where the mill once stood.

My mum and myself looked after our little farm, and the hours were very long, daylight till dark. The cows had to be hand-milked and then the milk water-cooled into large fifty-quart cans and taken to the gate for the carrier to pick up and deliver to the dairy. Any milk left over we separated for the cream. Mum and I hated turning that separator handle endlessly at 72 revs per minute to get the right thickness of cream. Then all the washing up of separator, cooler, cans and buckets and then sweeping out the cow bails. We always had a few chooks to feed and sometimes a couple of pigs. After all this was done, into the house for breakfast and then all the other chores around the house; washing clothes and household linen in the wood copper, wringing it all out by hand, then ironing it all with flat irons heated on the wood stove.

There are many incidents that happened in those days which had an effect on my outlook for life, but I think that the attitude that people had towards each other was really wonderful. Although we had very little, everyone was willing to help others in any way they could.

My husband was a very kind man and it used to worry

him to think of some of the local children not getting enough to eat. Much as he disliked to do it, he would kill a calf, skin it and salt the hide to take to the tannery and sell it to help our budget. Then he would cut up the veal, flour it and give it to families with a lot of children — and there were families of up to six and eight children. They would then bring their billycans and he would fill them up with separated milk. I always had chooks everywhere as I just loved chooks and chickens. There was always plenty of eggs, so a dozen would be put into a bag and sent along with the other goodies.

Whilst Harry was working at Strattons Mill, he would go up to Clifton Hill and buy a full side of mutton at Cook's butcher shop for two shillings and sixpence. He would also get a 25 lb bag of flour from the mill and I would make a pot of stew from the flaps and then put it into a large enamel pie-dish with a cup in the middle and cover with a thick puff paste made with butter. We always gave that to a family whose mother was very ill with tuberculosis and it always warmed my heart to see the pleasure on that mother's face.

The Depression taught us how to barter. Some of our neighbours were very good gardeners and they would bring their wheelbarrows over to us and fill them with cow manure, in return they would bring us vegetables. Many of the women would do sewing or unpick old jumpers and re-knit them in exchange for home-made jams, or honey as we had several beehives. Mum would make several batches of scones, and put in a few with the jam or honey. Also a little pat of butter (we always churned our own) to go with them.

Times were still hard in the war years. We were just slowly coming out of the Depression and the First World War was still very fresh in our minds, and we knew it was all going to happen again; the cream of our manhood was to face up to the same as their fathers before them, although the First World War was supposed to be the war to end all wars.

We were still struggling along farming and our third child, a son was born in 1939. My husband enlisted in the army.

With the help from my mother and a hired man, Ernie, we kept the farm going. It was really heartbreaking with so much to do and three children to look after. We would all be up at four in the morning, have the first shed of cows milked by 6.15 then a cup of tea, made in a billycan over an open fire, and a slice of bread and dripping toasted over the fire. (I can still taste that lovely first cuppa and toasted bread and dripping.) Then on with the milking to have the cans ready to be picked up by carrier at 9.30.

At 7.30 I would leave Mum and Ernie to go on with the milking and I would go and get the two eldest children's breakfast and see them off to school, give the baby his bottle and settle him off to sleep, then back to the cowshed and help to finish off the milking. After the carrier had collected the milk, back to the house and prepare breakfast for Mum, Ernie and myself, wash up the dishes, bath the baby, clean up, then bog into piles of washing in the wood copper, lift the clothes out with the copper stick and rinse and wring every-thing by hand. It would take about three hours to get every-thing washed and out on the line, when it was dry it all had to be brought in again, damped down and ironed.

We had one advantage, the butcher, greengrocer, and grocer would call and deliver three times a week and the baker every day. The fishmonger, with such beautiful fresh fish, called Wednesday and Saturday.

We all had our ration books with coupons for sugar, tea, butter, etc., and as we always had plenty of butter I would exchange my butter coupons with a friend for her tea and some sugar coupons. Petrol coupons were very hard to come by but being primary producers we always got a few extra and we just scraped by. Clothes rationing was harder to cope with as the children grew so fast and ours were not average size. Luckily we were given some extra ones for big children.

Towards the end of 1940 our fourth baby was born, another son. I became very ill with bronchial asthma which turned to pneumonia while I was in hospital. Our baby contracted pneumonia and died at the age of six weeks. I was so ill that my husband was discharged from the army on compassionate grounds. It was twelve months before I fully recovered and took up the threads of my life again.

We still continued our farming and I used to take our third baby up to the cowshed during afternoon milking. The older two would make his bottle when they came home from school and bring it up at 5 p.m. and feed him. They were a great help. Our little daughter would put the vegetables on and make the gravy, also keep adding boiling water to a steamed pudding. At six o'clock I would leave the bails and come in to make tea ready for us all. Then it was bath time for all and off to bed. Now that little girl is a wonderful cook and has taught her own two daughters and son the art of cooking.

My world fell apart with the loss of my husband in 1979, but now I have settled into an easy relaxed way of life. I am still an early riser and after a shower I take my little dog, Willie, for a walk. We do not go the same course every day but find new directions to explore. I take my string bag and call into the milk bar for my bread and milk then home to breakfast.

I belong to the Senior Citizens Club and also play carpet bowls, and look forward to Mothers Union meeting once a month at our church. I am a sidesman, which means I ring the bell, take the collection plate around and help count the money. Once a fortnight I visit old friends for a chat and a cuppa and on alternate weeks they come and visit me and we keep up with all the doings of old friends.

Weekends are always busy with family visits to me, or I do the rounds and visit them. Now I have more time in my garden and it is beginning to take shape, a very slow process and hard work. I am looking forward to the spring as I have put in some jonquils, freesias and snowdrops, wallflowers and primroses. Friends give me various cuttings and I am becoming quite expert at getting them to strike in pots. I am very pleased with it all as I didn't have time to mess about with plants when we were farming.

I now have six grand-daughters and one very big grand-son and they give me so much joy and pleasure. After a life of lots of hard work, happiness, hard times, joys and sorrows, I have settled down to a happy retirement with the help of my wonderful family.

Four generations

Ruth

Ruth Palmer b.1905

I was the second eldest of nine children, born and grew up on a farm in the south-west of Western Australia. By the time I was seven years old I was using a treadle sewing machine to hem sheets, teatowels and pillow slips. We all had our jobs to do and learned to milk the cows, feed calves out of a bucket, use the hand separator and help churn the butter.

My sister May and I never even thought of going out to work; we had quite enough to do at home with the sewing, cooking, entertaining, helping outdoors, etc. I don't remember the Depression except once when we took cattle up the west coast where a very big group of men were working on the diversion of the Harvey River. I still recall my amazement at the sight of these hundreds of men taking out barrow-loads of earth; it looked like a mighty ant track in the bush, all so busy with such small loads. The 'cut' they were making to the sea would have been at least ten feet deep: a tremendous task.

But of course the Depression did affect us. When we married in 1930 we lived in a small cottage on my husband's parents' property — it was sixty years old, the outside made of rough-hewn timber and the inside nicely lined with matchwood. This property was renowned for its good quality stone fruit.

In my ignorance I thought an orchard meant only summer work, picking and packing and hurrying away to the train with loads of cases. I soon found the winter days meant hours of pruning and spraying and ploughing before the reward of the blossoms: almond, stark white in mid-winter, followed by the pink of peach, then apricot, pear and apple and the small green fruit beginning to grow. In no time it's December; the first apricots and peaches are ready to pick and send to market. The fruit doesn't wait till you've nothing else to do — it ripens, it has to be picked: the early fruit usually brings big returns. Almost every day through the hot summer the work has to be done; once in a while a quick swim in the river to cool off. Orchards are so finely cultivated that a fine dust covers our feet. Some of the big old apricot trees would have been 30 feet across and usually a horse and cart would circle round slowly while the picker filled buckets or bags. We used to think that by the time you got back to starting point another lot was ripe — big luscious things they were.

Making fruit cases was a constant job and my husband, Beresford, was an expert: he could make a case in less than two minutes. We also started making furniture, mainly at nights. I would hold the lantern so that the light shone in the right place (no electricity then), working happily together, measuring, sawing, planing, cutting, and drilling hundreds of holes for morticing — my job through the day — until finally the glueing together and there was our lovely big kitchenette, still as good now as the day it was made, a large dresser, with its stained glass doors at the top, the two wide drawers and spacious cupboards. Since then we have made many pieces of furniture, from beautiful timber cut on the property, banksia, sheoak and jarrah.

I always intended to have a big family, six at least! In 1934 we built on the western side of my father's farm at Waterloo, buying 150 acres and putting in our dairy cows. But no babies arrived. I became the auntie who would take the littlies into my home while other mothers went to the hospital for a second or third child. I loved it, but my arms were empty when they went home. After seven years, though happy and healthy, we still had none.

A friend much older than I, told me, 'You need a child, Ruth. Do you realise that there are many babies who need a mother?'

I had not thought of adoption.

My husband said, 'It looks as though that's the answer. We could adopt a little boy. What'll we call him?' he asked thoughtfully.

Out of the blue I answered, 'Beverley.' He added, 'Robert.'

My mother was so pleased with the news that the following week she brought a parcel of baby clothes. My heart still swells with the joy of that first gift.

After a few months of correspondence with the Child Welfare department in Perth a telegram came saying that they had a baby that should suit us. With terrific excitement I made the long trip to Perth and waited in the reception room of the Home. Then Matron brought in the baby, fair, plump, and smelling gorgeous of fresh bathing and baby powder. I took him in my arms. Something was wrong, I felt no joy at all.

Bewildered, I said, 'He is not mine.' The two ladies looked at each other in amazement: 'We think he is lovely.'

'He is, but he is not mine. Haven't you got another little boy baby?'

They conferred for a few moments, then — 'Well, there *is* a babe, but he is not ready.'

I said, 'I don't care. Let me see him.'

After a short while they brought in the second baby. He had a wet nappy, sick on his dress and a rash all over his face. I took him in my arms.

Oh, what ecstacy! He was mine — without a doubt. I could barely find a place without a rash to give the first kiss to him. I asked the lady, 'What's his name?'

She said, 'Oh, he is called Beverley.'

My little son, with God's blessing.

Yes, that changed my life. I've never had a dull moment since. Later on we adopted another boy, Kingsley, and then much later, our daughter, Lois. Our family was complete.

Sylvia

Sylvia Jew b. 1901

LIKE Ruth of old I had to promise 'Whither thou goest I will go; thy God shall be my God . . .' At the Methodist Church, Caltowie, in South Australia I married Edward Jew, ordained Methodist minister, on 3 April 1924.

My great grandfather, Johann Heinrich Both, had arrived at Holdfast Bay in November 1838, took up land at Klemzig, moved to Reedbeds (now Lockleys) then to Lyndoch where he built the first water mill in South Australia to grind his corn. My grandfather, my father and his three brothers all became millers, and eventually my grandfather and his sons established the milling business of J. H. Both & Co. at Caltowie in the early 1890s.

My mother, Susan Louisa Richardson, born the same year as my father in 1865, migrated from Bermuda with her parents in 1877. Besides their own eight children they brought three nephews as well and the voyage took six months. Mother married my father, John Henry Both, in 1890 at Burra. They had five daughters and three sons. I was the fourth daughter. They were wonderful loving parents, staunch Methodists, and I never remember one saying a cross word to the other.

After high school I attended Methodist Ladies College and in 1918 I sat for the Senior Commercial Exam in the Exhibition Building in North Terrace, Adelaide. It was the

morning of 11 November. I shall never forget the din as we made our way down North Terrace. Car horns were tooting continuously, people were sitting on bonnets of moving cars waving flags and shouting.

Those two years at MLC made a great impression on me. Miss Patchell the Head, was a fine Christian woman who led prayers each night before 'Prep' and also gave us a Bible lesson on Sunday afternoons. She often took the older girls to concerts in the Town Hall and elsewhere to hear noted musicians and vocalists. Then I was needed at home in my father's office at the mill, and there were two more of the family to go to boarding school.

Ted Jew came to Caltowie in 1921 and had been there for quite a long while when I realised that when I went to the post office each morning at 9.30 he was often there, too. So began our interest in each other.

In 1923 he was appointed to the church in Waikerie, and a stone manse was commenced soon afterwards. This was of four rooms with a wide passage from front to back door. A verandah shaded right around the house. At the back, part of it was enclosed for the kitchen (with iron!), and the other corner as bathroom and laundry. The copper for heating the water and boiling the clothes was right outside.

It was the Methodist Church custom to furnish the manse and to provide house linen, cutlery and crockery. In this way a minister and his family could be moved more easily from one circuit to another, and with less expense. On our return from our Melbourne honeymoon we found ours at Waikerie furnished with good secondhand furniture and we were thrilled. That was the year ministers began providing their own house linen and cutlery so I didn't ever have to use bedding and linen that someone else might not have taken care of.

Ted had a motor bike for transport and I could go only walking distance. Ramco, Taylorville and Lock Two were also in his care. With few cars about we were fortunate when one young couple used to leave their horse and buggy in our care when they went on holidays.

The Bishop family lived on one side of us and the Donhardts with several children on the other. Whenever either of us went outside the back door, Mrs Bishop would be waiting to have a chat. Her men folk went off in early morning and she'd never had close neighbours before but we always wished she had more to keep her indoors.

A number of single men had taken up fruit blocks and were glad to have meals at the Donhardt home. Two boarders there used to come into our home at any hour of the day as they had nowhere to spend their leisure time. Reg used to use our piano and Jock built himself a crystal wireless set and put it up on a small table in our dining room. It was hard to keep the exposed workings free from dust.

Ted conducted a wedding service in his study once, and the couple walked down the passage to the dining room as Reg played the Wedding March on the piano. They were thrilled. Then we had a cup of tea and some refreshments together before they went off to their new home. They seemed so old to me to be just getting married: probably in their fifties.

Their little cottage was on the river bank, two rooms with

an iron roof. They invited us to spend an evening with them, which we did. There was only one chair and a table in the room. Ted and I were given boxes to sit on. The husband (I can't remember his name) sat on the chair and Paulina on his knee. We were having supper, eating the cake that Paulina proudly announced had five eggs in, when suddenly there was a shower of rocks on the roof, a terrible din, and both of them rushed out shouting. I was really scared. It was some of Paulina's nephews and friends showing that they knew they were married!

Paulina used to go each day to meet her husband after work so that he wouldn't go to the hotel and drink. Then she started drinking with him. The last we heard of them was that she had left him and he was glad she'd gone.

In 1925 our first baby, John Edward was born. Then we moved to Clarendon in the Adelaide Hills. Often Ted would walk over the hills to Cherry Gardens to take an afternoon service there. Then a gift from my parents, and he went to Adelaide to take delivery of a new blue Overland car. He had never driven before but he drove it home. But I had to back it into the shed!

Now I was able to go with him on the circuit — Kangarilla, Cherry Gardens and Reynella besides Clarendon. Instead of being paid with the usual monthly cheque, Ted would come home from the quarterly meeting with a bag full of three-penny pieces — the actual ones that had been put in the collection plate. A Methodist minister was never paid a very high stipend so we never had much to spend.

We often spent a day in Adelaide, an 18-mile (29 km) drive. Ted loved books and bookshops and soon built up his library. He always stayed up late reading. Kerosene lamps were used then for lighting, so we bought an Aladdin which had a mantle, so he could have a good light. Whenever he went home to Melbourne his mother would give him money to buy books, explaining to me that they were his tools. I never objected anyway. If Ted and his brother Henry happened to be home at the same time they would have a wonderful time haunting bookshops and coming home laden with bargains.

In June 1928 Lorna Margaret was born, and by this time I knew a bit more about babies. The old house at Clarendon had plenty of room for a family and the Ladies Guild had provided money for a new carpet for the sitting room and the suite was re-covered with moquette. We found that wherever we lived in the country there were wonderful staunch people and we always hated to leave so many good friends to go to a new home.

After three years at Clarendon we went to Hallett, in the middle North, very open country and very cold in the winter. There had been a drought the year before and the countryside was very dry. Even though a well and windmill were in the backyard there had been no wind to pump the mill and so no supply of water for the lawns and gardens planted by our predecessors. This was about the beginning of the Depression.

We were very short of money as people could give only what they could spare for the church. Often we would have men call and ask for food and we always found something to give them. I remember John asking one, 'Are you a faggy?' Another man asked, 'Does his riverence have an old flannel shirt to spare?'

Some of these men were regular callers and we were told that many of them went up and down the railway line nearby and called each time. They camped in the recreation ground and by some means let others of their kind know at which houses to call. They never called next door to us, but did at the next house where they were given tinned fruit and other good things. Sometimes the farmers would bring us some meat, and these were not all church people. Sometimes we were given wheat for fowls' feed so we were really very well off. Ted now used a motor bike instead of the car and so we managed.

A young couple who had never been further north than Adelaide came to visit us. Clarrie was in Wesley College hoping to go into the ministry later. He had conducted a service at Abattoirs and was amazed to see two-shilling pieces in the plate. He thought threepenny pieces were church money!

The Ululoo gold diggings were about 10 or 11 miles out from Hallett. Years earlier a quantity of gold had been found there, and now quite a number of unemployed men camped there hopefully. There was a man called Fletcher who walked in each week carrying a sugar bag over his shoulder and he'd call in at the manse for a chat — and some refreshments. Ted used to go out to the diggings occasionally to see how the men were faring.

We took Clarrie and May out to Ululoo and near by, where the men had been digging, was a deep dry creek with a sandy bottom. The children were playing happily there when all of a sudden we heard a terrific roar and a few drops of rain came down. We dashed down and carried the children up the bank and then the flood and rain came. Further out there had been a terrific storm. We sheltered in a small iron hut. And soon we saw huge tree trunks hurtling down the flooded creek, just as if they had been matches. When we set off for home and neared Hallett we could see the town surrounded by water. We were glad to get home safe and sound that day.

Mrs Bayley who lived two doors away began having pasties delivered to the manse. We enjoyed them, but then a big piece of fritz (beef german) began to arrive twice a week. We enjoyed that too, but it was so continuous that we could not manage so much. John was only six and Lorna three so they were not much help and even Lassie the dog was not so keen. We couldn't say we didn't want it and offend the old lady who was so generous because she heard that the minister was having a hard time. Wherever we lived there were wonderful people.

The south-east town of Millicent was our next home: a large circuit with much travelling — Tantanoola, Kalangadoo, Hatherleigh and Beachport. The Mount Burr forests and mills were just opening up.

One thing we had to contend with was fleas. The previous occupants owned a dog and dogs' hairs clung to all the bedside mats and hearth rugs. We were told that fleas bred in the sandy soil there. Before we went to bed we would throw back the covers and search and usually exterminated a few. But at last we could have a good sleep without any searching.

Ann, the Church of England minister's daughter, was Lorna's friend. One morning they were just outside the study door and I heard Lorna say, 'Let's go in and ask Dad for a penny. He's more kinder than Mum.' The school tuck-shop was right across the road.

Elinor Mary, another blue-eyed baby arrived in 1933 and when she was two we were transferred to Gumeracha in the Adelaide Hills. Now in an apple growing district we had plenty of fruit and we also kept a cow which provided ample milk for our growing family. The manse was quite a large one but it needed repairs. The ceiling in the sitting room was badly cracked and looked as though it might come down any time. And it did! One Sunday night I heard a clatter and thought something must be falling on the supper dishes. Next morning we saw what it was. About two tons of plaster.

By the time our youngest child was born I had much to keep me busy, with the cow to milk when Ted was not home, the separating and then making butter as well as everything else. There was plenty of fruit always ready to be made into jam and desserts; we never lacked a dish of thick scalded cream to go with them. Vegetables grew easily so we were well provided for, and the butcher, baker and grocer called.

One hot windy day in January 1939 a fire broke out at Kersbrook racing through the hills towards Gumeracha. We had to think quickly. We let out the fowls and cow, took the bath outside and filled it with water, and decided if the fire actually reached us that the church next door would be our best refuge. Ted had John blowing up the tyres on the car in case it was needed — but it wasn't.

Our next home, Yongala, was in drought when we arrived. Ted always said, wherever he was sent there was always plenty of work waiting to be done. It was a small town — one general store, a few smaller ones; a butter factory which closed that year; the usual churches and hotels, a post office and a bank. It was the coldest town in the State. One morning I woke to find a thick blanket of snow all around us and on the hills in the distance.

The house was a solid six-roomed building, but no mod. cons. We just had a wood stove and the bathroom (?) was an iron structure outside the back door, against the kitchen wall. It contained the wash troughs and copper and an old wooden washstand with an enamel bowl and the bath by the wall facing the back door. This wall (iron) was just as high as the door — the top area was open to the elements. I remember being in the bath with the rain splashing in on me — in those temperatures! John rode his bicycle to Peterborough High school eight miles away and I always had to rise very early to get the family off to school; no electric jugs in those days.

In the grip of drought the dust storms coming down from the north were horrific. Often so dark, we would have to light a lamp in the daytime and the fowls would roost at 3 p.m. Big flocks of sheep would sometimes come through on their way to better pastures and small lambs, unable to keep up, often got left behind. They were taken care of by the townspeople and John, too, brought one home. When it grew big it had to go to the butcher — who promised not to let us have any of our lamb.

Port Pirie, again, was unlike anywhere we had ever lived. An industrial town, with the Broken Hill Associated Smelters the chief source of work, it hardly provided ideal living conditions. If there was a north wind the fumes from the Smelters would settle right over the town and woe betide any garden. It looked as if it had been scorched by fire.

The circuit consisted of Solomontown, Warnertown and Broad Creek. Religious instruction began in state schools and Ted had to be out at Warnertown by 9 a.m. Mondays. Then the Port Germein circuit with Mombray Creek and Baroota were added to his load. Petrol rationing, due to the war, had begun and he had all these extra miles to travel. Every third Sunday he took six services, travelling long distances. He, of course, was happy in his work and enjoying the busyness. I also took a class for RI (religious instruction) at Solomontown school on Friday afternoons; so few people would undertake this work. As there was also a branch of the Comrades (a club for teenage girls and young women) and a Ladies Guild I was kept busy. We never knew when there would be extra to a meal or someone to stay the night.

RAAF servicemen from the near-by flying station brought wives and children from interstate to live in rented rooms and houses, and some came to church services. We held a sing-song for them after the evening service followed by supper. Other young people would come to me as well and how I used to provide all this supper with food rationing I just don't know, but these little gatherings kept them in touch with the church.

Living in a manse brought us all kinds of callers for all kinds of reasons. Ted used to have meetings nearly every evening and on a free night would often visit the hospital. One visitor that we had was 'Squarey' Farrell, an alcoholic whose cousin told us not to have anything to do with him as he was an awful man. But Ted was sympathetic towards anyone in trouble. Once he invited Squarey to tea with us and while we were all eating that meal Squarey told us how he made his escape from Gladstone gaol. That evening he went along with the others to a meeting at the church — but came out halfway through. On a Saturday afternoon I saw Ted and two friends and Squarey standing in a circle in the back yard with bowed heads, praying. Talking about it later one friend said that as soon as he opened his eyes again he felt to see if his watch was still there.

The Sunday school anniversary was a great event. All the girls had new summer frocks to wear although only yet August. There were so many children up on the platform they helped keep each other warm. One of the Sunday school teachers used to come in a broken down trotting sulky and would sometimes give me a lift — we sat up high with the horse trotting fast as it could, and to think of it still makes me laugh.

Then, as always, the four busy years passed, and we moved to Gladstone in 1945. Looking back, it seems to me, my role in wartime was 'to keep the home fires burning', and that kept me very busy indeed.

Some people may think that as I am in my eighties that life would be drab and uninteresting, but I do not find it so. Certainly my way of life has changed from earlier years but still the weeks fly by, and I never seem to have time to do all I plan to do. That is probably because my movements are slower.

I usually wake early and have my devotions then. Gardening fills some of my time and my garden (a small one), especially my roses, brings much pleasure. Patchwork, tapestry and reading (I like biographies) are more spare time activities. Keeping in touch with my family help fill many hours with letter writing. Friends near home, especially those who are sick, I contact by telephone. Thursday I attend the 'Over Sixties Forum' in the city, Sundays the Uniting Church and its Day Fellowship once a month, and the Hallett Girls Gathering bi-monthly. These, and the meetings of ministers' wives, renew friendships, some going back for over fifty years.

When my daughter said to me, 'Why don't you enrol for the "Write About Your Life"' course, I replied, 'I've never done anything exciting, or been anywhere, what could I write?' But it was a challenge and just the stimulus I needed to get me going after an illness in 1980 when I had wondered whether I would see my eightieth birthday. I have been amazed at the memories that have come flooding back, and it has not all been easy to tell.

215

Epilogue

In the process of writing their stories the authors began accruing unexpected benefits. They were not only 'putting a house in order', they were also extending it.

Meg Oliver wrote:

'. . . I was feeling that I needed something other than doing offerings for stalls and charity things. I have a lot of friends who still correspond but time slowly decreases that pleasure — in my age group friends do drop out. Actually, my "better half" conned me into it.

'I seem to have lived my life all over again and feel much better in health for doing so. So much of my life I had to accept sorrows and hurts and hide reactions for fear I upset others. Well, I have brought things to light and re-acted as I should have done. My husband often found me tear-stained and would say, "Ah! Writing about your life, I see."

'When he started to read without correcting my spelling and punctuation, I began to think I was doing a fair job. With the gentle criticisms I received and Guy's encouragement the project has been a continual joy.'

There is no way of describing Meg's zany letters that cheerfully chatter on with loads of humour and few full stops, covering the past, present and future on any subject from the Roman Wall to her latest acquisition, a knitting machine.

'. . . To date I have done a dozen little baby coats, in spite of ravels and flying antennae when I forgot to hold the wool. I think I am slowly getting somewhere.'

Interspersed between reminiscences of the past are merry commentaries on the weather, the flu, a dire electricity strike, Guy's vertigo, the Avon lady, the home help, the delivery boy, family affairs (she is a step-grandmother) and the old Settler's Home that was sawn in half and disappeared in the night. She types because her hands are 'rheumaticky'; she has pernicious anaemia and broke her hip in a fall three years ago and mentions the problems of none of them. Guy gets frustrated because his world 'keeps going round' and he can't drive or work in the garden any more but, judging from the number of friends, relations and neighbours who drop in for a talk, tongues are in fine fettle.

Others reported a similar reaction in improved health. *Dorothy*'s daughter Elsie appended a letter to her mother's work in which she said,

'The course has caused my mother to remember all sorts of things which she had never told me about before, and it has enabled her to see a pattern to her life and the context of it which she has been most delighted to discover.'

Alice found a bonus added to her reading — this was also noticed generally.

'. . . Whenever I read a book or an article now, I go back over something which strikes me as special, wondering how ever such a piece of prose was conceived or written.'

Perhaps she had in mind the poem she enclosed that had

been given her by a neighbour who died in 1980 after reaching her 100th birthday.

> *Washing Day — Three Generations*
> In grandma's day, washing was a job
> That no-one envied.
> A bench beneath a shady tree
> Tin tubs she had to empty.
> She drew water from a well
> Or carried buckets from a near-by spring
> Then boiled her clothes in a kerosene tin
> Yet you seldom heard her grumble.
>
> By mother's day things had improved
> To a wash-house and built-in copper
> With concrete troughs to suit her height
> And taps to turn on water
> And they really thought when they had all that
> They had everything they ought to.
>
> Now her daughter has a fine washing machine
> A spin-dry for a wringer
> A clothes hoist at the very back door
> That really is a winner.
> She presses a button and turns a switch
> And hey presto! she's finished.
> The washing's all up on the hoist to dry
> And she's hardly had time to begin it.

(Composed one day by Mrs Janet Nasebandt when she was watching clothes on a hoist spinning in the wind. © Nasebandt family)

Joan discovered herself.

'. . . Now I know that I AM ME! Something that I didn't realise until recently — and no matter what others do to try to change me, like attacking me for being stuffy and old hat, etc., etc. I can't change now, too late, and to be honest I like me as I am. And apparently quite a few of the younger kids think I am *great* — in modern talk that is quite some word isn't it? Some poor kids these days just haven't a clue what fun it was to live when things were so much more free. This sounds silly seeing that the permissive society has taken over, but our lives *were* free in so much that we didn't get stuck with the same bloke year in and year out before we eventually married — we had fun and games with various ones, learnt to judge character. When I told my niece that I had been engaged twice before I did marry, she said, "How ever did you get hold of *three* men?" We had a tennis court at home and had lovely tennis parties, nobody partnered with the same chap every Saturday either. I once went to a party in the house described in *Diaries of Ethel Turner*. When I showed the book to J. she exclaimed, "Goodness me! Surely you weren't alive *then*?" You can imagine, I felt like a ghost from the past.'

Eileen and *Sandy* discovered each other.
The stories told in turn by each indicated their paths might have crossed. Had they ever met? They had indeed. They had nursed at the Westminster Hospital together. In no time at all a reunion was arranged.

'. . . You should have seen us walking towards each other when I went to meet Sandy and Smithy (another ex-colleague). I felt sure it must be them, but oh! how they had changed — and I could just read the expressions on their faces which said, "Do you think that is *her*?" But it didn't take us long to slip into our old (or young) skins and forget the almost fifty years that had passed. The chit-chat went on non-stop all afternoon.' *Eileen*

'. . . It was almost a Rip Van Winkle story, almost too much to bear. Smithy took a bottle of dinner wine — we didn't need it. Later we were joined by L., another of the old crowd. It was all "Do you remember . . .", "Will you ever forget . . ." It just went on and on.

'We used to have a tiny room where the steriliser was housed — we had a slate there for messages — Smithy would write up:

GOD SAVE THE KING

Healy (Eileen's maiden name) would come along and write:

DE VALERA FOREVER.

One would write a line of verse and the next one in would add to it. They were wonderful days. Then Smithy and I went to Carnarvon and I hadn't seen Healy since we left Westminster and that would be 1935.

"How ever can you remember all these things," L. said, "I don't remember any of it." But as she had entered a convent for a time she probably spent a lot of it praying.'
Sandy

Sandy afterwards joined Eileen in attending Trinity School for Seniors in Perth.

'. . . On the first day I sat in at the Literature class and found myself out the front giving a talk on Vera Brittain.' (This may not seem special but in Sandy's cover letter with her first assignment she had stated, 'I never knew there were books other than nursing textbooks.')

Ellinor, a little frail now, put her story together with the help of her daughter Margaret who could only visit on alternate weekends. Margaret contracted polio many years ago and is confined to a wheelchair but works in Administration at the Royal Melbourne Hospital. They enjoyed their project so much they are currently working on another through the Hawthorn Community Centre. Ninety-three is no time to give up.

There have been feelings of real achievement. Whole books have been completed, either printed privately for families or waiting hopefully to find a publisher. But *they have been written.*

Retracing the past can be risking disillusion with

somewhere loved long ago, then that too, becomes new experience.

Thora has since returned to Sweden and England, twice; notwithstanding a colostomy operation which she once thought of as 'the worst thing that could happen to anyone' only to find 'there are hundreds of us. I would howl buckets of tears under the shower trying to keep clean, but thank the lord, I manage better now.'

Catherine and Terry attended the 40th Anniversary 'D Day' Celebration in Portsmouth Cathedral on 3 June 1984:

'. . . We made our way to Portsmouth at the end of May and had great difficulty getting accommodation as the city was, even then, bursting at the seams. But before the big day, we made our plans to get to the church at Wymering-Cum-Widley. 1 June was very wet and the area round the church seemed unrecognisable as, like most other places, fields have been overtaken by houses. Inside, it was as beautiful as 1 June 1945. People were busy doing flowers at the altar as there was to be a wedding the next day. In order to encourage the young couple, we wrote in the Visitors' Book:

Catherine and Walter Pearce-Shorten,
married in this church,
39 years ago today.'

Eileen, after taking lessons in Beginners German, flew off to Germany to visit her daughter and family, then on to Ireland to rejoice among myriad relations — and her brother Pat.

Families just keep on growing and the larger they grow the greater the distance they spread, and visits extend interstate and overseas. Someone is always going somewhere to stay with a daughter, a son, a grandchild. There are great grandchildren by the dozen. The pride and the love and the sense of belonging is manifest. The true joy is in the belonging.

COMING OUT!
WOMEN'S VOICES,
WOMEN'S LIVES

Edited by Julie Rigg
and Julie Copeland

A selection from ABC radio's Coming Out show

The programme has been controversial, irreverent, angry, unexpected, compassionate, funny, couragous. It reflects a wide range of subjects and an even wider cross-section of women. There are programmes on feminist elements in *Alice in Wonderland*; Western man's obsession with breasts; women farmers' battle for recognition; romantic fiction and pornography; abortion reform . . . The programmes speak for and to women — and men as well!

Germaine Greer: 'My Life since *The Female Eunuch* has been a disaster area, and it's getting worse . . .'

Doris Lessing: '. . . when the men go away the women instantly create a kind of hedonistic, permissive, indulgent world where they try on dresses, cook, gossip and have a lovely time.'